FOR THEIR TRIUMPHS AND FOR THEIR TEARS

Conditions and Resistance of Women in
Apartheid South Africa

by

Hilda Bernstein

Remember all our women in the jails
Remember all our women in campaigns
Remember all our women over many fighting years
Remember all our women for their triumphs, and for their tears

(from 'Women's Day Song')

International Defence & Aid Fund
104 Newgate Street EC1
Revised edition May 1978

First published 1975
Revised edition 1978

The International Defence and Aid Fund for Southern Africa has the following objects:-

1. To aid, defend and rehabilitate the victims of unjust legislation and oppressive and arbitrary procedures;

2. To support their families and dependants;

3. To keep the conscience of the world alive to the issues at stake.

ISBN No. 0 904759 22 9

CONTENTS

An Explanation and Some Essential Information

The language of apartheid is a totally necessary part of its ideology. Without the special words and phrases that have been created, the ideology would disappear, because it is not a theory constructed on the basis of reason, but an expedient developed to disguise the truth and erected on the basis of a special language.

The opponents of apartheid are forced into a semantic trap: once you begin to use the language of apartheid, you have already accepted something of the premise. Yet it is impossible to write about South Africa today without using some of this special, and totally misleading, language.

For example, apartheid speaks of South Africa as being divided into White areas and Homelands. The White areas are more than 87 per cent of the total country, while the Homelands are less than 13 per cent, mostly scattered areas which are not even consolidated into the nine designated Homelands.

This is historically a lie — the demarcation is something imposed by White government — and factually nonsense, since the majority of black people actually reside in the 'white' areas. But these are terms used by government spokesmen, and in fact must be used when quoting from them; so that eventually some people have come to accept the idea that 70 per cent of South Africans are entitled to live in only 13 per cent of the land area   their 'homelands'. On the other hand, it can be cumbersome always to condition these terms by using quotation marks, or prefacing them with 'so-called'.

Apartheid has also developed words and phrases that have meaning only within the context of apartheid — for example, 'Bantu', or 'Separate development', or 'Endorsed out'.

What follows here is a brief explanation of some of the apartheid language, to make this book easier to understand.

HOMELANDS, BANTUSTANS, RESERVES: These all refer to the areas that successive white governments have designated for occupation by the Africans. **Reserves** was used in the past, and today has more accuracy inasmuch as these areas have become reserves of cheap labour. **Homeland** is the official term, reflecting the intention of the white government. **Bantustans** originated as a satirical term, and is generally used by opponents of apartheid. In 1961 Dr. Verwoerd, then Prime Minister of South Africa, frankly stated that 'in the light of the pressure being exerted on South Africa' the government would introduce new Bantu states, 'a form of fragmentation which we would not have liked if we were able to avoid it, thereby buying the white man his freedom and the right to retain domination in what is his country'.

5

SEPARATE DEVELOPMENT: This is the preferred official term for apartheid. It is intended to emphasize the idea that racial separation is based on separate development, and to avoid the unpleasant ideas associated with the term **apartheid.**

BLACKS, BANTUS, AFRICANS: Bantu has been the official term used for Africans, who dislike it as being inaccurate and offensive. **Black** covers three racial groups, that is, Africans, Asians and Coloureds (the term used in South Africa for people of mixed white and black extraction) and, as well as being adopted by the black people, is now coming gradually into official favour.

BLACK SPOTS: These are areas of land occupied by Africans that are surrounded by white-owned territory, or are 'poorly sited', that is, too close to white farms or towns. To clear the 'black spots' massive uprootings of settled populations and communities have taken place.

INFLUX CONTROL: A mass of regulations and legislation has been evolved for the purpose of restricting the number of Africans entering, residing or working in urban areas. Influx control is carried out by the labour agencies, by police, magistrates' courts and the Bantu Affairs Department. It is achieved by means of the Pass Laws.

PASS, REFERENCE BOOK: The pass laws which restrict the freedom of movement and choice of occupation of the African people have their roots in the beginnings of white occupation. Every single African male and female over the age of 16 years must carry a pass at all times and produce it on demand. On average nearly 2,000 people every day are prosecuted for infringements of the pass laws. In 1952 the various laws controlling movement were consolidated into one Act, enabling the authorities to issue reference books to Africans in lieu of the various passes they were formerly required to carry. The book contains the holder's identity card as well as particulars of residence, employment contract, tax receipts, etc. In addition it contains endorsements regarding the eligibility of the holder to live in, work in or seek work in prescribed areas. 'Passes' and 'reference books' are therefore interchangeable terms.

SECTION 10: This is the section of the law (the Bantu Urban Areas Act as amended) which lays down that no African may remain in prescribed (that is, 'white') areas unless he produces proof that:

(*a*) he or she has lived there continuously since birth; or

(*b*) he or she has worked there continuously for one employer for at least 10 years, or has lived there lawfully and continuously for fifteen years, and has not been convicted of a serious offence and has not been employed outside the area;

(*c*) he or she is the wife, unmarried son or daughter under the age of 18 of someone in the above categories: or

(*d*) he or she has been granted special permission to be in the area.

People with these residential rights may be ordered out if deemed to be idle or undesirable. Up to 1964 wives were allowed to live in urban African townships if their husbands qualified, but since then there has been an effective embargo on the entry of women to the urban areas other than on a visitor's permit for a specific period. The wording of the regulations suggests that exceptions may be made, but couples who apply for the wife to join her husband find that in practice permission is not granted. By removals and other means, the number who qualify under Section 10 is being steadily reduced.

ENDORSED OUT: An endorsement in the reference book means that the owner of the book must leave a prescribed area (that is, one considered to be white, but where a large number of Africans live and work).

BORDER AREA, BORDER INDUSTRY: Where it is possible, white industrialists have been encouraged to build factories in regions adjacent to a Bantustan. This policy has a twofold purpose: to use the black labour of the reserves while keeping the workers essentially based in the reserves; and to de-centralise industry from the four main industrial areas of the country. The idea is that black workers will live within the reserves in 'towns' sited along the borders, cross over to the 'white' area to work during the day, and return again at night. In fact many Africans employed in border industries must travel to and live in the vicinity of such industries, and are therefore still migrant workers, although the burden of providing them with accommodation is shifted to the Bantustans.

BLACK SASH: An organisation of predominantly middle-class women (whites only until 1963) who have become known everywhere through their silent protests against many apartheid laws, wearing a black sash. In recent years, the organisation has devoted most of its attention to the evils arising from migrant labour and mass removals, and conducts advice offices in Cape Town and Johannesburg to which Africans come with problems arising from the laws. They publish a magazine, *The Black Sash*, and are deeply concerned at the destruction of family life.

POPULATION OF SOUTH AFRICA: An official estimate in 1974:

Africans:	17.7 million
Whites:	4.2 million
Coloureds:	2.3 million
Asians:	0.7 million
	24.9 million

CHAPTER 1

Women Under Apartheid

Women in South Africa suffer first and foremost from the disability of apartheid.

South African society is built in layers in which class and colour coincide. The position of South African women corresponds to their skin colour: the white man is at the very top; at the very bottom of the pile is the black woman.

White women share the right to vote at all levels with white men, and in general their position may be equated with that of women in many other male-dominated societies. Despite their privileged position they do suffer inequalities in employment, wages, and in law; but they also enjoy the inestimable advantages that go with a white skin in South Africa.

A vast superstructure of custom and law, in which the habits and institutions of an old, pastoral society are cemented into a modern industrialised state, rests on the backs of the black women of South Africa. Black women suffer additional disabilities both in law and in custom as compared with black men. Some of these are rooted in the past; some are similar to those suffered by women in most countries throughout the world, relating to inferior job opportunities, discrimination under the law, and many unjust forms of discrimination at all levels.

A crucial factor in the position of the women of South Africa has been that of the impact of imperial power on an indigenous culture. Inferiority was imposed on the African peoples by the nature of colonialism in Africa. But the woman has the burden doubled: the black consciousness of 'inferiority' ingrained by the colonists, the destruction of tribal structures that gave status to both sexes and the denigration of any culture other than that of the colonists themselves is the first imposition; the second is the inferior status imposed by the relationship of the women and men.

And overlaying all this is the unique structure of South African society which does not only discriminate against women as such, but reduces African women in particular to the very lowest status, virtually stripped of rights and of opportunities to improve their position. Over and above this they are also stripped of those things which are considered basic rights throughout the world: that is, the right to live with their own husbands, the right to bring up and care for their own children, the right to lead any normal kind of family life.

The laws that do this to African women are in the first place the special laws of apartheid. A brief explanation of the apartheid basis is thus essential. It is not possible to start to understand the conditions and problems of the black women of South Africa, their needs and the necessities for change, their status and their demands as women, without first understanding the overriding factors which mould and control their lives, rendering all other women's problems of a secondary nature.

Apartheid is a totally divisive society, one in which the emphasis is always on the differences between people, and these are elevated above those things that people have in common. Superficial differences, such as the amount of pigment in the skin, assume a created importance, and become the visible outward signs of inequality. Life roles are laid down at birth, by skin colour and by sex; education, achievement, status, jobs, are thus predetermined, and if the child questions the role into which she has been cast, then she will find there is no way to change it save by changing the whole society. This applies to the males as well, but because of their totally deprived status, it applies most forcibly to the black women, who are cast in a role so demeaned, so subservient, so totally lacking in any expectations of achievement, advancement or independence, that it seems a miracle for any of them to develop beyond the function of reproduction and domestic work.

Furthermore apartheid was in the past, and is today, a policy of privilege based on the desire of the politically dominant white minority to maintain a system of intensive exploitation, racially based. In the post-war world, however, apartheid's advocates have been forced to adopt an ideological stance in order to justify before the world community a very blatant form of racial discrimination which is no longer acceptable, particularly in an Africa emerging from colonial bondage.

The ideology proclaims that South Africa is not one but ten separate nations. One of these nations is white and totally skin-defined; that is, all white people regardless of language, origin, culture, belong to the white nation, and this includes English-speaking and Afrikaans-speaking white South Africans as well as those of other origin, including recent settlers from Greece, Italy, Germany, Portugal and other European countries. The blacks, on the other hand, constitute nine different 'nations', determined largely on the basis of language: they are the Xhosa nation, the Zulu nation, the Swazi nation, the Venda nation, and so on.

This enables the Nationalist government to pretend that their policy is not racial, 'but based on the reality and the fact that within the borders of the Republic there are found the White nation and several Bantu nations. The Government's policy, therefore, is not a policy of discrimination on the grounds of race or colour but a policy of differentiation on the ground of nationhood of different nations, granting to each self-determination within the borders of their homelands — hence the policy of separate development.'[1]

Geographical separation of these ten 'nations' is said to be necessary so that each can preserve its ethnic identity, values and way of life; and restoration of the traditional culture of each is essential for this goal.

This calls for a policy that is fundamentally different from that of former colonial periods, which sought to destroy indigenous culture; instead apartheid publicly states that it wishes to preserve traditional law and tribal customs among the black 'nations'.

Apartheid claims that the white 'homeland' constitutes 87 per cent of all South Africa, taking in all the cities and major towns, the areas of industrial development; all the mines and ports, the main rail and road networks. And that the Africans — 70 per cent of the population — must develop their 'homelands' in 13 per cent of the country, the reserves, the Bantustans, some 280 blocks of land, many of them small and isolated tracts; all of them lacking urban centres, industries, infrastructures, important exploitable mineral deposits and sea ports. Most of them are eroded and overfarmed, and — even if developed to their maximum — unable to support the populations assigned to them.

But that, in effect, meets the needs of apartheid. For the ideology of separate development and the maintenance of white supremacy must go hand in hand with rapid industrialisation and maximum growth in the 'white' areas. The considerable growth in the past, in the present, and as planned for the future, relies absolutely on the plentiful supply of cheap black labour. Just under five million Africans now live in the 'white' towns and a further three million work in 'white' rural areas. Only seven million — less than half of the total black population — live in the 'homelands'. [See Appendix, Table I]

South Africa may claim the unique distinction of having the only government of modern times which is deliberately dismembering a unified country. In this attempt to unscramble the different strands that make up a nation already long consolidated by its industrial development, vast population removals have been carried out, and more are planned.

The size of these transfers of people is also unique in our times — not less than three million out of a total population in 1970 of 21.45 millions.[2] It is impossible to say how many more will be caught up in this process by the time the full programme of removals under various apartheid laws has taken place.

The contradiction between geographical separation and economic integration is resolved by a spreading pattern of migrant labour. Increasingly all black workers are being turned into migratory workers, as all blacks living within the 'white' homelands must be regarded as temporary sojourners, permitted to stay only as long as they can be usefully employed by the whites.

The extended migratory labour system is operated through the application of the pass laws, and these mesh together with the uprooting and removal of people, singly or en masse.

These three policy-factors — that is, the pass laws, migratory labour and population removals — deeply and devastatingly penetrate the daily lives of the women of South Africa.

CHAPTER 2

Migrant Labour — The Breaking of Families

To achieve its primary position of wealth, strength and power, South Africa has drawn on and required a constant supply of cheap black labour.

Post-war Europe is familiar with the phenomenon of migrant workers leaving their own country to work in another for a specified period. There are such migrant workers in South Africa as well, 367,000 of them who come from other African states to work in the mines, leaving their families in their own countries and ultimately returning to them. These fall outside the scope of this book, which is confined to the internal migrant.

In the distorting mirror of apartheid, all black workers outside the reserves are migrants who leave their own 'country' to work in white South Africa — a different country. This precept is now being applied not merely to those workers from rural areas who seek employment in the towns, but also to those settled communities of black families who have often been town-dwellers for two or three generations.

Migrant labour, as other communities have found to their cost, has an adverse effect on family life and social development, as the men who should be playing their part as husbands, fathers and members of the community are absent for long periods. Where such dislocation is temporary and small-scale the effects may be remedied but in South Africa the intention is to turn the entire black work force into migrant labour — permanently.

There are still in existence large black townships serving the towns and industries, notably Soweto outside Johannesburg, where workers live with their wives and young children. But in other such townships — Alexandra, also outside Johannesburg — all family housing has been destroyed, wives, children and old people despatched to 'resettlement' camps in the reserves, and hostels provided for 'single' black workers. "We are trying to introduce the migratory labour pattern as far as possible in every sphere", stated a prominent Nationalist MP, Mr G.F. van L. Froneman, who later became Deputy Minister of Justice, Mines and Planning. "This is, in fact, the entire basis of our policy as far as the white economy is concerned."[3]

It is estimated today that half of the African labour force in the urban areas are migrants. They are not seasonal labourers, but part of the grand design of apartheid by which the inherent contradiction between an ideological theory demanding race separation, and the needs of a developed industrialised economy requiring a constant supply of cheap labour can be reconciled.

Migrant labour causes the destruction of family life and turns human beings into units of labour to be manipulated at will, while wives and children become unnecessary dependants who must be removed from the urban areas where they serve no purpose for the white economy.

In 1969 Mr Froneman named the conditions under which 'foreign labour' (that is, South African blacks) could be used without conflicting with apartheid. Among them: no rights of domicile or citizenship in the white homeland. And *"This African labour force must not be burdened with superfluous appendages such as wives, children and dependants who could not provide service."*[4]

"We need them to work for us," stated the Prime Minister, Mr B.J. Vorster, "but the fact that they work for us can never entitle them to claim political rights. Not now, nor in the future . . . under any circumstances."[5]

"It is accepted Government policy that Bantu are only temporarily resident in European areas as long as they offer labour," said an official circular from the Department of Bantu Administration (12 Dec. 1967). "Bantu in European areas who are normally regarded as non-productive and have to be resettled in the homeland area are: (*a*) the aged, the unfit, women with dependent children, squatters on mission stations, etc; (*b*) professional Bantu such as doctors, attorneys, industrialists."

The official term, 'temporary sojourners', is applied to African workers who are integrated with, and an integral part of the country's economy. They are allowed to work in that economy because it would collapse without them. But they are not regarded as human beings. A resolution passed at the 1973 Congress of the Afrikaanse Studentebond (Afrikaner students' organisation) demanded that "All the black women and children in the white area be shipped back to the homelands and only the men should be left in the white areas for as long as we need them."

Other aspects of the official view are no less inhuman. "We do not want the Bantu women here simply as an adjunct to the procreative capacity of the Bantu population."[6] A wife should be allowed into the town only if she were needed on the labour market. Her husband could visit her from time to time.

This official concept of family life for the blacks — where husband and wife normally live apart but the husband may sometimes visit his wife — is under-lined in a circular from the Department of Bantu Administration and Develop-ment to local authorities in 1969. The circular put forward the proposition that where a (white) town is close to a 'homeland', the Africans employed in that town should actually live in the 'homeland'. Should the distance between town and 'homeland' be too great, however, hostel accommodation should be provided for the workers in the urban areas, who should be able to visit their families periodically.

When the Black Sash wrote to all South African churches stating that since the church preached the sanctity of marriage and family life they should protest against official policy, the largest of the Christian Churches the Nederduits Gereformeerde Kerk (Dutch Reformed Church) replied, "That families in many cases cannot live together is true but it is also true that they are granted the opportunity to visit each other — provided of course they are willing to comply with the relevant regulations and they do not disregard this privilege."[7]

In *Migrant Labour in South Africa*, Francis Wilson says that the migrant labour system is based on the premise that a human being can be broken into two parts: a 'labour unit' working in town, separated from the other part, a man with a family, with hopes and aspirations. "If man was seen primarily as a human being who among other things was a worker, then such exclusion would not be possible."[8]

In the special language of apartheid, blacks are not ordinary human beings. They are labour units, who are productive or non-productive; who are temporary sojourners in the towns even though they may spend their whole lives working there; or illegal immigrants within the borders of their own country; whose wives and children are superfluous appendages — non-productive, the women being nothing more than adjuncts to the procreative capacity of the black male labour unit. Only through this process of de-humanisation is the application of inhuman laws possible.*

Migrant labour exerts a powerful force on the lives of South African women. The system itself makes it virtually illegal for the majority of African women to live with their husbands, except during the annual two-week holiday when migrant workers may go to visit their wives in the reserves. It makes a mockery of family life, cutting an impassable chasm between husband and wife.

Official statistics about the marital status of South African women of various races tell their own story about the social consequences of the migrant labour system. According to the results of the 1970 census there were more married white females (843,000) than there were unmarried (837,940). Married white women as a proportion of all white females (1,870,360 — including widows, divorcees etc.) constituted 45% of the total. In contrast, amongst Africans, married women (2,153,860) constituted only 28.2% of all females (7,649,020), and were less than half as numerous as those who were unmarried (4,740,300).

Migrant labour is the most important single factor in the life of South Africa, affecting the lives of every single person living in the reserves, a large proportion of all workers in urban areas, and indirectly the lives of all South Africans, black and white. During the long periods of their youthful, sexually active lives, husbands and wives must live apart. For many, a family unit is never formed. The result is social chaos.

Francis Wilson sums up the evidence of his research on migrant labour with a devastating list of 31 arguments against it, including many that touch directly on the lives of women. Among others, it aggravates and creates illegitimacy, bigamy

---

*When some 800 African men were moved from the tops of blocks of flats where they had rooms in the buildings where they worked, to men's hostels 12 miles away, the official proclamation said that 'superfluous living-in Bantu males' were to be accommodated in hostels, and a women's hostel would be built for 'superfluous living-in Bantu females'. (*Rand Daily Mail* 30.10.69)

13

and prostitution; homosexuality and drunkenness; breakdown of parental authority; malnutrition, tuberculosis and venereal disease. Together with influx control and mass removals under 'resettlement' plans, migrant labour is depriving millions of black women of the most elementary and fundamental rights, and creating the conditions for untold tragedies.

The position of women is thus determined by apartheid's labour policies. Regarded as 'appendages', they are denied an existence as human beings with abilities, aspirations and needs of their own. And their way forward is doubly blocked: as 'appendages' their role is limited and cannot be changed while they are debarred from all but the most menial and economically insignificant forms of employment, chiefly in domestic service and casual farm labour. The status of women can only undergo a fundamental change in South Africa when the migrant labour system is abolished and when women are able to take part on equal terms in the economic life of their country.

CHAPTER 3

Forced Removals — The Uprooting of Millions

The mass removal of population takes place under various apartheid laws with the basic aim of separating the four main racial groups into different compartments, and of further separating the Africans into their nine ethnic 'nations'.

Under the Group Areas Act, which is designed to segregate the other three races in 'white' areas, 600,000 people have been moved, of whom the majority, over 550,000, are Indian or Coloured.

Africans are removed under laws designed to clear up the so-called 'black spots' — areas occupied by Africans in territory now designated as being 'white'. Large-scale removals have taken place under the law which makes it illegal for Africans to live on white farms as squatters or labour-tenants — estimated as nearly one million by 1973.[9] Under influx control laws another 400,000 people who are redundant to the needs of the 'white' economy have been endorsed out to the re-settlement villages or other areas in the reserves. More removals are taking place under proposals to try and consolidate the scattered land areas of the reserves.

In 1969 the Deputy Minister of Bantu Administration Dr P.J. Koornhof, told parliament that the removals so far carried out were a tremendous achievement.

"We have labour, peace and stability amongst the Bantu who are performing essential work in our white areas. We are also affording our industrialists that stability in order to enable them to use Bantu labour for the performance of essential work . . . But those Bantu in our white areas who are not economically active and are not engaged in the performance of normal or good work, should be channelled back to their own homelands . . . Approximately 900,000 Bantu have been settled elsewhere under the Nationalist Party regime over the past few years, since 1959. Surely this is no mean achievement; on the contrary, it is a tremendous achievement."[10]

It is an 'achievement' which hits black women most of all. Some African women may stay in the towns to work as domestic servants. "There are single African women who could be usefully employed in the White areas", said Froneman, "and, while there are white families who could not do without domestic help, the moment a Bantu woman starts a family, then she belongs in her homeland."[11]

It is impossible to describe adequately what forced removals, both individual and mass, and the systematic break-up of family life have done to the women of South Africa. There is no complete study, official or otherwise, of the mass removals of populations and the consequent splintering of families. It is not even known for certain how many people have been uprooted — the figures are always estimates. But some idea of the extent of this uprooting is contained in the figures: 15% of the total population forcibly removed or shortly to be removed — and this is by no means the end.

Whether they are moved singly, or as part of a group from farms or 'black spots', each removal is an individual tragedy beginning with the stonewall of an official decree and ending in the destruction of home and family.

The act of removal itself can be a bitter and terrible experience. From homes in towns where there were some amenities — schools, shops, transport, industries, clinics; or from lands regarded as ancestral where the enlarged African family could thrive in all its warmth; to arid settlements in distant places they must go, the 'unproductive units' or the 'idle and undesirable', the chronically sick, the too old and too young, and the wives and widows, deposited in Limehill, Sada, Welcome Valley, Mdantsane, Dimbaza, spewed off Government lorries with what possessions they are able to take . . . and left to resettle. In countryside which is often grotesque and desolate, they will be taken to a few rows of un-shaded iron or asbestos huts without floors or ceilings, or to inadequate tents. They are uprooted, then flung down on the most inhospitable soil, and left, if it is possible for them, to find roots and to go on living. But it is those who are least able to cope with the trauma of the removals — families without menfolk, the old, the ill — who form the majority of those resettled. Bewilderment strikes to the very roots of the soul; apathy in the face of problems too great to overcome; sickness, decimating those least able to resist; death. These are the most dispossessed people of our times. The burden is carried by the women.

They have lost, or are losing every day, homes, husbands, sons, children, the place where they were born or have lived the longest and know the best; the community from which they drew friendship, assistance, strength; the familiarity of known streets and houses, even if the surroundings were poor. There is no way to compensate for this, *even if* — and the opposite is true — even if the substitute had a form materially better than the one left behind; even if there were better houses, sanitation, amenities, the dispossession would still be there. They have been robbed of what was theirs, the known and understood, the landscapes that seep into the mind's eye, the circle of neighbours and the cycle of domestic events and patterns of intercourse that even the poorest societies construct around themselves. It is as though they must begin the whole of their lives all over again, but now under totally alien and hostile conditions.

Because most of the resettled are 'superfluous appendages', whether from the urban locations or from 'black spots', these people must be resettled on land which neither now nor in the future will be desired or needed by the whites. And because of the overcrowding and endemic land hunger in the reserves, the resettlement camps are sited in the places even the local Africans avoid, where the earth is iron-hard so that even the digging of latrines becomes an insuperable problem; where there are no natural features to enhance the value of the land, no grass, trees, crops; far from the white settlements, therefore lacking roads, telephones, doctors, schools, social and other amenities. The people are, literally, thrown away.

The physical setting is usually harsh enough. But more difficult to assess is what happens to people so treated. Ferdinand Mount writes about "the sense of dispossession": "The political and the psychological permeate and reflect one another. The loss of home, the resentments of physical exile, the deprivation of the familiar things and relationships which give meaning and relish to life, these shade into the less material sense in which we say that a man feels he is an outsider, a stranger, an alien."[12]

Bruno Bettelheim, concerned about the human condition in mass society, describes the "Muselmänner", the walking corpses in Dachau, who were those who had come to feel that their environment was one over which they could exercise no influence whatsoever.[13] They were people so deprived of affect, self-esteem, and every form of stimulation, so totally exhausted, both physically and emotionally, that their environment had total power over them. To each of these his own life and environment were viewed as wholly beyond his ability to influence them.

A mission doctor in South Africa describes the problems of women who bring babies to hospital suffering from malnutrition: "A mother may become infuriatingly inert and difficult to help because the struggle seems so hopeless. Often she struggles on — it is uncomfortable to picture the sort of scenes where distracted women try to comfort hungry children in empty huts scattered through the reserves . . . Eventually she is driven to leave her children with whoever will have them and go to the towns to work for them."[14]

In this way are the black people of South Africa brought to their homelands. "You cannot be brought home against your will," says Mount. They come to a life of extreme poverty and hopelessness from which there is no way to break out. Activity is weakened by malnutrition; there is no money for mobility and no means of earning it. In any case, there is nowhere else they may legally go.

CHAPTER 4

African Women in the Reserves

There are four million African women living in the 'homelands' — the reserves. They suffer disabilities in virtually every facet of their existence, an existence to which they are bound by a complex interlacing of tribal and common law, together with the fact that, unlike the men, they are less able to escape by going to the cities. For more than a decade influx control and pass laws have prohibited black women from taking up lawful residence in the cities and the urban areas.

Black women in the cities are subject to many of the same disabilities that affect the women in the reserves; but in the latter there are some differences and added disabilities arising from the distortion by white governments of customs and laws of a former society. The insistence of apartheid that what they call the indigenous culture of the people must be preserved in the homelands leads to contradictions that cannot be resolved today — any more than the clock can be turned back to restore a former type of society — and it is the women who suffer most from the anomalous situations.

Quite apart from the problems of trying to maintain tribal structures and laws in an advanced industrialised state, the government has made a parody of tribal institutions, keeping the form but removing the content.

The retention of the system of chiefs, for instance, is necessary to apartheid theory and administration. In the past, chiefs governed always with a council of tribal elders, a method that was traditionally patriarchal but not wholly undemocratic, although it excluded women and younger men. Today the chiefs are not heads of tribes who take decisions after long discussion with the elders; they are simply appointed civil servants, deposed if they do not carry out government orders and policies, and the council of elders no longer exists. In its place, the chief has headmen, whose role is to maintain "law and order", as laid down by official policy.

Many other features of traditional African cultures, such as the absence of a money economy, or limitless cattle grazing, are in total conflict with the requirements not only of an industrialised society, but also of apartheid. So the apartheid-created homelands have a specious version of African custom and tradition imposed on them, and to these the people must conform.

This version, states sociologist H. J. Simons, reflects the authoritarian and patriarchal attitudes of the whites who devised it.[15] In particular, it incorporates many restrictions on women which are totally out of keeping with their modern attitudes, education, situation and needs — restrictions which, if they did exist in an earlier era, existed in conjunction with other rights or safeguards that white legislators, administrators and judges now ignore.

Perpetual minors

Women are virtually perpetual minors under African customary law. They cannot own property in their own right, inherit, or act as the guardian of their children. They cannot enter into contracts, sue or be sued, without the aid of their male guardian. Regardless of their age and marital condition, women are always subject to the authority of men.

This is how customary law has been interpreted and applied by white courts. But it does not truly reflect the position of women in the tribal society. "Women had more rights as regards both their person and property than have been conceded to them by alien courts . . . Common law terms such as ownership, contract and status itself are saturated with an individualism alien to traditional African culture. Unless elaborately qualified, they distort the social relations underlying African legal rules. It would be closer to the mark to say that there was no law of contract, or that ownership was unknown in tribal society, than to draw a distinction in these matters between the capacity of women and men."

Initiative and the right to act rested with the family rather than the individual. There were clearly defined positions for each member, with claims and obligations, but the household constituted an integral whole. Neither man nor woman could normally exist outside a domestic group, and the activities of the sexes were complementary and not in conflict.

"A woman shared her father's or husband's rank. She undertook much of the laborious work in the home and fields, not for an employer but for a family to which she and her children belonged. What she produced or acquired did not become the 'property' of her husband. It formed part of a joint family estate which he managed, not in the capacity of 'owner', but as head and senior partner."

Women occupied a subordinate position, even though they might attain a high degree of independence in some roles, such as those of diviner and herbalist, and occasionally in some tribes as chieftainess.

Each sex had its own sphere of activity, and women did not contend with men for power, rank or office because their roles were not competitive.

The concept of the independent woman cannot take shape in this kind of society, where there is neither class war nor the battle of the sexes. People see themselves as members of kinship groups, not as individuals with separate rights. "Something more than legal reforms is required to emancipate women from the patriarchal authority. The family must cease to be the main productive unit, and lose its self-sufficiency, women must receive modern education and participate, along with the men, in productive activity outside the home, before they can assert claims to equality of status."

Today, even in the reserves, many women live outside the bounds of tribal society. Migrant labour and influx control regulations force them to become the heads of households; they must act often as wage-earners as well, and all over the country are widows, divorcees, women whose husbands have disappeared, and unmarried mothers. Yet customary law as it has been institutionalised by whites places them perpetually under male tutelage, creating tremendous hardships. The contradictions that arise from this grafting of an old skin over a new framework place an intolerable burden on the whole African people, but most severely on African women.

The status and rights of married women in the African reserves are determined by complicated rules arising out of tribal law as interpreted by white judges and administrators and as affected by common and statute law. Laws affecting domestic relations vary from province to province; the most regressive, reactionary and repressive features of tribal law as codified and construed by the white regime are incorporated into the notorious Natal Code (Law No. 46) of 1887.

Africans in both town and country may choose to marry according to general South African law — 'common law' — or according to tribal law — 'customary unions'. Marriage by common law is more usual in the towns; most Africans in the reserves marry according to tribal law, that is, customary union.

African women must have parental consent to enter into a customary union. Such marriages are validated by *lobolo*, the transfer of cattle and/or money by the husband to the wife's father. In its earliest forms *lobolo* was not a bride-price so much as a 'child-price', whereby the cattle exchanged gave the husband claims to the wife's children as his own. Even if the marriage broke up, the claims remained valid, voided only through the return of the cattle.

While some aspects of *lobolo* served a useful function in providing protection for married women, it had an essentially retrogressive aspect, curtailing the independence and freedom of women. The wife who wished to leave her husband found it difficult to do so because rights to children were involved. Men who had come into ownership of cattle or children were not inclined to part with them merely because a woman wanted her freedom, and the only alternative left to the woman in the absence of a cattle refund from her father, was to give up her children. Even today, an African man may repudiate his marriage unilaterally simply by forfeiting his *lobolo* rights, but an African woman has no equivalent right.

Lobolo was thus one of the means whereby women were under the dominion of men in traditional society. This is worth stressing, for there are those who believe that the problems lie wholly with white misinterpretation of tribal laws and customs and who would welcome a return to principles embodied in customs such as *lobolo*. But for women there can be no return. The struggle is against apartheid, which holds all in bondage, and also against all retrogressive traditions that deny women full rights over their own lives and equal treatment under the law.

An African woman married by customary union is considered a minor under the tutelage of her husband. She cannot own property in her own right, except for her clothing and a few personal possessions; and if she earns money or in any way acquires property this becomes the property of her husband.

These laws vary somewhat according to the province. In Natal for example, custody of the children can never be given to their divorced, separated or widowed mothers, even if it is the husband's conduct that caused the marriage break-up. Elsewhere, a divorced woman is deemed to have reached her majority, but in Natal a divorced woman is a perpetual minor, once more subject to the control of father or guardian, and she must live in his kraal. Her ex-husband keeps the children, though they must be allowed to stay with their mother until the age of about six.

Any woman may be confined to her kraal by a banning order issued by a Bantu Affairs Commissioner if he finds that she 'leads an immoral life', or being absent from her kraal is unable to give a good account of herself.

An African woman married by customary union is generally unable to own property in her own right; unable to make a valid contract without her guardian's consent; or to sue or be sued. Her husband must do this on her behalf.

The Minister of Bantu Administration and Development told Parliament that one of the aims of his policy "was to restore women to their rightful place as wife, mother, leader . . . the position that women occupied in the old society."(16)

"In the name of restoring African women to their rightful place in that society, this specious culture over-emphasizes restrictions on women and distorts their role in rural society," says Elizabeth Landis. She concludes: "Since various rights denied to African women under the Natal Code or married according to tribal law are granted without disastrous consequences to single women, it is apparent that these rights are not withheld for the protection of African women. However, to concede this would be to challenge the validity of the separate culture imposed on Africans — and, more importantly, to challenge the concept of separate culture as a basic tenet of the South African political system. The Government consequently cannot countenance any fundamental amelioration in the status of rural African women, for such a reform would inevitably undermine apartheid."(17)

Land hunger

Women also suffer from the land hunger endemic in the reserves. The lack of sufficient land to support the population has been aggravated by the 'resettlement' in the reserves of Africans who have been brought from the cities, from the 'black spots' or white farm areas.

It should always be remembered that the term 'resettlement' does not usually mean that the Africans brought to the reserves came from there in the first place, or have ever been to those places in their lives. Most of the people in resettlement camps have been born and lived all their lives in urban areas or other parts of the countryside. Dumping them into the reserves increases the problem of insufficient land. But the local authorities are able to ignore a large proportion of such problems by their refusal to allocate land to women.

By law, allotments of land may be made to any married person or kraalhead who is officially a citizen of the particular reserve or 'homeland'. A widow or unmarried woman with family obligations can be defined as a 'kraalhead', but the allocation of land is an administrative act that cannot be challenged in a court of law. Only a widow with children has any chance of being allocated land, and usually she will receive only half of the allocation made to a man.

A widow in occupation of her late husband's land forfeits her right to use the land if she remarries, or leaves her late husband's homestead, or refuses to live at another place agreed by his family. This condition ties her rigorously to the allotment, and induces widows to enter into relationships rather than forfeit land rights.

A widow is expected to find money to pay for quitrent and local tax, and buy food and clothing for herself and her children, out of the produce from the land, which may be no bigger than one or two acres. If she assumes the role of breadwinner and leaves her children in the reserve to go and work for a wage, she runs the risk of losing her right to cultivate her holding.

Women in peasant communities cannot exist easily without land or father, husband or son to support them. The preference given to male kinsmen often imposes severe hardships on women who are passed over in favour of a brother or nephew of a deceased holder. "An obvious solution would be to allow unmarried daughters to use the plot in the absence of a male descendent, but the administration objects that this reform would make girls independent of male control and place a premium on 'spinster motherhood'. It is official policy to buttress the patriarchal authority. But the main course of the objection is the chronic and acute scarcity of land."[18]

In the Transkei (the largest 'homeland') land scarcity, states Simons, is the major determinant of policy. Women do most of the work in the fields; yet the administration insists that they are less productive, so widows get half the male allocation. But throughout Africa, the women have always been the cultivators; they, and not the men, are the true producers.

"But the main argument is the shortage of land and the need to provide land for men with families. The people reply that the country is full of widows, and ask how they are to support their children without land. The widows pay taxes like the men, and should have the same rights as men to change their place of residence. The people complain that the administration oppresses widows . . . There is often bitter competition between individual men and women for land, but the conflict stems from land hunger and not from tribal custom. The people want to restore to women the rights they had to land in the old society. But all attempts to bring about the change have failed to persuade an inflexible bureaucracy which is not responsible to the people."[19]

Lack of jobs

There are few jobs for women in the reserves, who are barred from seeking work in the cities. They are frequently less mobile than the men, with household responsibilities that cannot be discarded, and widows are afraid to leave their homesteads to seek work as they will then lose rights to cultivate the family land. There are virtually no secondary industries and little other work, apart from domestic service, for poorly educated women. The small number of women who can find employment mainly work as labourers or domestic servants on nearby white farms. Others obtain seasonal farm work. A very few find jobs in the two professions open to them, nursing and teaching. In recent years some 'border industry' jobs have been created in some parts of the reserves. These jobs, usually in small-scale craft or textile production, are done by women at the lowest end of the wage scale, receiving less pay than men would get in the same job and less than blacks in similar work in the industrial centres. The vast majority of African women in the reserves, however, cannot find paid employment and must rely on money sent by men working in the towns to supplement their meagre subsistence cultivation.

Loneliness

The typical more fortunate woman in the reserves has a husband working in the city while she attempts to feed the children, and probably other dependents, on the crops she cultivates from the small, barren family plot, if any, and the meagre amounts, if any, that are remitted by her husband — if he does not take a city wife or fritter away his small pay in other ways during his long absences. And this housewife, virtually a widow from the time she marries, lives out her lonely life, unable to leave, in a community composed largely of women, children, the aged and infirm who have been endorsed out of the cities once they become 'unproductive' labour units.

An African woman writes of the women of the reserves: "It is the tragic story of thousands of young women who are widows long before they reach the age of thirty; young married women who have never been mothers; young women whose life has been one long song of sorrow — burying one baby after another and lastly burying the husband — that lover she has never known as husband and father. To them — both men and women — adulthood means the end of life; it means loneliness, sorrow, tears and death; it means a life without a future because there is no present."[20]

In the barren and particularly unproductive resettled areas, women may spend most of the day collecting firewood and carrying water from the nearest river or borehole, just to sustain day-to-day existence.

Poverty

The lack of job opportunities in the reserves and the extreme poverty leads inevitably to sickness and death. Kwashiorkor, scurvy, pellagra and beri-beri are rife; tuberculosis and other diseases associated with malnutrition and poverty are widespread. Deaths from starvation, particularly among children, are common. The Government does not keep full mortality or morbidity statistics for Africans, as it does for all other sections of the population, but infant mortality rates in the reserves are known to be very high.

The plight of the children in remote reserves is even worse at the camps in the resettled areas. Dimbaza, one of these dumping-grounds for expendable humans, was first described by a Catholic priest, Cosmas Desmond, in his book *The Discarded People*. He wrote:

"One look . . . was sufficient to convince me that the reports I had heard had not been exaggerated and that there was grinding poverty, squalor and hardship equal to the worst places I had seen. There were families, tiny one roomed houses, many with a number of ragged, hungry-looking children or a bent old woman sitting outside. It was not quite true that I could no longer be shocked or disturbed. I was, in particular, by the sight of one tiny baby, a virtual skeleton, unable to move or even to cry and covered with flies. I have been through children's wards in African hospitals throughout the country and, over the past ten years have seen thousands of starving, dying children. But I doubt whether I have seen anything worse than this. It was as bad as any of the horror pictures from Biafra."[21]

By May 1969, although most of the inhabitants of Dimbaza had arrived only during the six months previously, there were already over 90 graves, 70 of which were those of children. In January of 1972 (high summer in the Ciskei) there was much gastro-enteritis and in less than two months, 52 children died. By the beginning of May 1972, there were over 400 children's graves. Confirming these figures, a government spokesman regarded them as being nothing unusual.[22]

The diseases of malnutrition are likely to cause physical or mental stunting — or both — for life, and the children who survive the disasters of such a childhood grow up to reinforce white myths about the limited initiative, intelligence or work ability of the blacks. But it is official policy that causes the malnutrition.

24

CHAPTER 5

Women in the Towns

The assumptions of developed societies that people should be free to choose their own partners in marriage, live with them, enjoy some stability in family life, quite apart from the wider assumptions regarding education, housing, social services and old age pensions — all these are totally contrary to the pattern of life for women in South Africa.

The problems raised by marriage are enormous. Any African woman who was born in the reserves, who marries a man who is qualified under Section 10 to live in an urban area, may not normally live with her husband. She may apply for permission to live with him, but this is rarely granted. Her husband can, of course, visit her during his annual leave. If, on the other hand, she is qualified to live in an urban area under Section 10, and she marries a man who is not qualified to live in the same urban area, then she is immediately endorsed out — expelled to the reserves.

A woman fortunate enough to live a family life in an urban township such as Soweto must avoid the misfortune of being widowed or divorced — if she is, she will lose the house and be endorsed out. Her hold on her own home is thus tenuous, and the supply of such limited family housing can never equal the needs, because it is government policy to restrict the provision of such homes.

Local authorities have been warned by the Deputy Minister of Bantu Administration not to provide urban Africans with "bigger, better, more attractive and more luxurious facilities, because it should be remembered that an urban Bantu residential area is not a homeland but part of a white area. When these facilities have the effect not only of making the Bantu accustomed to a foreign taste, but to enslave him to a luxury which his homeland cannot afford, and thereby alienate him from what is his own, then it is time to revise our sense of values."[23] He said a stage had probably been reached where the provision of housing for Bantu in white areas would have to be restricted, and he stressed that "the Bantu should come to the white areas for no other reason than to convert their labour into cash."[24]

In this process of converting their labour into cash the Africans have generated tremendous wealth for white South Africa. During the recent years of economic boom, a little of the prosperity has washed against a very small proportion of the African people, creating in the large township of Soweto outside Johannesburg a tenuous and limited middle-class.

The husbands are small businessmen, or journalists, or work in advertising agencies or with insurance companies. They drive new model cars, have homes with substantial suites of furniture, and go on holidays to the special segregated black camps in the Game Reserve, or to the beaches reserved for them in Natal and the Cape. The wives adopt material standards, follow the latest fashions, have tea parties, arrange flowers. For this tiny minority it can be said that materially their lives have improved, even if they live in segregated townships, carry passes, and may never enter the 'white' cinemas and theatres.

The majority of African women however have had no share in the prosperity which they and their husbands and sons have helped to create through their cheap labour. They know only low, inadequate wages, poor housing without water, electricity or privacy, insufficient medical facilities, and all the other wants that go with poverty. Over and above this they suffer from the insecurity that penetrates every aspect of their lives, making the right to keep a job or a home, the right to stay with a husband or child equally uncertain — no right at all.

Residential rights

Fewer women than men qualify for residence in urban areas. Many women fail to qualify under Section 10 (see introduction) because they have spent disqualifying periods elsewhere; many women, for instance, go to parents in country areas for the birth of babies. Because relatively few black women have been integrated into the country's economy except as domestic servants, they have been less likely to spend the necessary time to qualify under Section 10, either with one employer or by continuous residence in a town. Domestic servants are likely to change their place of employment fairly frequently, either because this has been the only way to obtain a higher wage, or because their periods of employment have been interrupted by child-bearing.

Women who have come to the towns and have not been able to qualify for residence may stay only until they are found out. There is no way in which such women can legalise their position. Marriage to a man who qualifies for town residence does not alter the woman's position. If she does not qualify, and he does, then there is no way in which they can legally live together as husband and wife. Frequently the husband does not qualify for residence in the same area from which the woman has come, therefore even if he could find work there, he would not be permitted to live with his wife. Many women who might qualify under Section 10 are unable to produce sufficient evidence to prove their case.

An unmarried daughter who qualifies for residence in an urban area through her parents loses that right if she marries a man from a different urban area. She cannot, however, go to live with her husband, as she is prohibited from entering another urban area.

African women who are living lawfully in an urban area may only obtain work through the municipal or district labour officer, from whom they must obtain a permit. Labour officers can refuse to issue a permit for many reasons, or they may refuse a permit for a specific job that a woman wishes to take and refer her to another somewhere else; or they may require women, with their dependents, to leave the area. A labour officer can also cancel an existing labour contract, a provision that hangs over the head of those African workers (male or female) who may participate in trade union or political activities.

Elizabeth Landis states that particularly when out of work, an African woman must avoid any activity which would make her fall within the definition of an 'idle Bantu' in Section 29 of the Urban Areas Act. That definition includes any black woman other than a 'bona fide housewife' who is between 15 and 60 and who, even if supported by her parents, is normally unemployed although capable of working (unless she is a student). It also includes women who refuse jobs offered by the labour officer, or are fired too frequently. A person held to be an 'idle Bantu' is ordered to be removed from the urban area.

A black woman must also avoid conduct which will lead an urban authority to hold her presence was 'detrimental to the maintenance of peace and order' and therefore make her liable to removal. This would seem to include participating in strikes, persistent complaining, and involvement in political movements.

Every African woman is painfully aware of the official attitude repeatedly expressed, that married women, children and older people are 'superfluous appendages', to be removed from the urban area as quickly as possible, even if they are technically qualified under Section 10. Single African girls, it is grudgingly admitted, may be useful in some cases, but once an African woman marries, she should go 'back' to the reserves.

A work permit may also be refused to a woman if she is unable to find housing, and the women are under severe difficulties as houses are not usually available for women. Hostels and compound accommodation is for men (with the exception of the Alexandra hostels). Women are now prohibited from being registered tenants in the townships which means that women who have lived in a house legally with their husbands become homeless if widowed, divorced, separated or deserted, and face immediate eviction. A black woman states "It is a sin for any mother to lose her husband in our urban areas. Some officials demand that the widow must come to their offices a day after the funeral of their husband to discuss the question of the house . . . The widow is not entitled to the tenancy of the house."(25)

If a widow qualifies to remain in the urban area independently of her late husband, then she may be given a lodger's permit, but her children and dependents will be sent away to the reserves.

Many unhappily married women suffer, unable to take any action, knowing that if their husbands desert or divorce them, they will lose the right to live with their children as well.

An African woman is even subject to arrest for living with her husband if he stays with her in domestic servants' quarters, or if she cohabits with him in his quarters when he is not qualified to have his family with him.

Because of the large numbers of men living in hostels, young women and girls in urban areas become the victims of unstable relationships.

"Mothers are harassed and embarrassed by the perpetual pass raids that take place in our locations. Mothers are never sure of finding their husbands at home because if they forget their passes they are never given the chance to produce them within a certain period. They are locked up and it usually takes days to trace them. Boys and men are usually grabbed at their own gates and refused permission to fetch their pass in the house. Men are handcuffed and marched to a police station for such minor offences. This lowers the dignity of the man and humiliates him."(26)

The laws which control the residence of black women in the 'white' areas are being more and more forcefully applied as the drive to abolish black residence rights outside the Bantustans intensifies. The brutal destruction of people's homes in the 'squatter camps' around Cape Town which took place in 1977 and 1978 was largely directed against women who were defying the government by establishing unofficial dwellings and communities where they could live as families with their husbands and children. Official policy is to reduce African 'family units' in the Western Cape, and compel women to move to their 'homeland' (chiefly the Transkei Bantustan). Women are thus sent off by train while their menfolk are directed to 'bachelor' hostels, and the homes they lovingly constructed and furnished despite poverty and adverse circumstances are savagely bulldozed and burnt. In many cases the families refuse to be split, and move off to build new homes in other squatter settlements. So the demolitions continue.

CHAPTER 6
Family Life

The devastating effects of all this on family life cannot adequately be described.

The privileged children, says Dr Trudi Thomas who worked for eleven years in one of the homelands, the Ciskei, are those who are cared for by their mothers and can look forward to regular registered letters at the post office with money to provide them with food and clothes and school books. They also get a share of affection, even if only from what is virtually a one-parent family. Others are not so lucky. Their parents' marriage begins to crumble under the stresses of separation. Bonds of loyalty and responsibility weaken, a man may stop sending money home. He is away from his wife for long periods of their most sexually-active life, and not unnaturally the husband may form a new relationship in the towns while his wife, also, if it is available, may find some small comfort and companionship from someone else.

The women in the towns who form relationships with men from the migrant labour force may be married or unmarried (married women who go to work in the towns seldom have the privilege of living with their own husbands). Many women migrants, writes Dr Thomas, have been deserted by husband or boy friends, others have been forced to turn bread winner through the death or sickness of their menfolk. Most have children in the reserves who are their sole responsibility to sustain. Frequently they must also support aged parents.

There are also young, single women seeking to escape the boredom and grinding poverty of the reserves.

Jobs and infants are incompatible. Husbands who see nothing wrong with impregnating another woman expect their wives to remain 'faithful' to them. Women may be left to give birth to unwanted babies without any attendants. Infanticide is a socially acceptable and tautly 'hushed up' solution.

The illegitimate baby may be brought up by old grandparents, but in any case is too often only a liability, a calamity. Between 30 and 70 African babies of every 100 born in big towns are illegitimate (59 to 64 in Durban, 50 to 68 in East London, 67 in Pietermaritzburg).[27]

"These are the Children of Resentment. *And deprivation.* Deprived of affection and sufficient food. Having no birthrights nor privileges nor status. Lacking discipline (only reviled). Denied self-respect. Nobody notices them nor praises their triumphs. Nobody comforts them, nobody cares. Unprotected, unstimulated, untutored, unoccupied, left to their own devices.

"Deprived, too, of example. They have no model of home life, nor of the roles of husband and wife and how they ought to treat one another, and what parents should do. The knowledge of these things is not instinctive, and so quite simply

29

these children do not learn to behave decently . . . If you set out, deliberately, for the sake of behavioural science, to produce a vicious and brutish person, you could hardly pick a better set of deprivations."[28]

Soon there is another category of illegitimate children, the children of children, and as a result of their brutal circumstances of life, they have brutal values. Thus the net of the pass laws, migrant labour and resettlement camps produces something else: the psychopathic personality, basically indifferent to the sufferings of others, lacking in any personal sense of understanding or remorse for their own acts, unable to form any sort of stable relationship, and lacking in any understanding of how other people feel.

"Broken marriages and desertion and faithlessness are distressingly common, and the reason is clear. It is fundamental to realise that African relationships, as in all cultures, depend on loyalty and affection. These bonds in turn depend upon mutual support and comfort, on shared experiences and responsibilities, and companionships. All these must be sacrificed when the man goes away for long periods, becoming virtually a visitor to his own home. Many ties come undone. Human relationships are very sensitive and separation makes them very vulnerable, and provides a fertile ground for faithlessness, jealousies and suspicions, accusations, real and imagined. These lead to shattered relationships which cause great misery; in relevant interviews people often express great bitterness and seething resentment, which may spill over into all their inter-personal relationships. Unloved, they become unloving; neglected, therefore neglectful; unsupported, therefore unsupporting . . . Migrant labour selects and reinforces brutish attitudes, callous and irresponsible behaviour."[29]

Children are illegal

While the black woman may be able to serve a useful function in the economy as domestic servant, both in town and countryside, (and to a limited amount in service and secondary industries in the cities) the black child is totally useless as far as the white regime is concerned, the most superfluous of all the worker's appendages.

Children who live with their mothers in the urban areas may not begin school before the age of seven, and then they must go to the right ethnic group school. It is government policy to reduce secondary schools in the urban areas, so that parents who want their children to have education above the primary school level are forced to send them to the homelands for their schooling.

When they reach the age of 16, to stay in the towns children must be registered on their parents' permits, but many of them are not so registered. Sometimes the authorities simply refuse to put a child's name on the permit; sometimes mothers are unable to produce a certificate showing the child was born in the area. Registration of African births is not compulsory; and where mothers are illiterate they may often be ignorant of the provisions that will ultimately govern their children's lives. An illiterate mother who is given a form to fill in by the local clinic, which would be evidence in years to come, may ignore it; or the child may have been born at home, without assistance except from neighbours, whose verbal evidence years later will not be accepted. Sometimes the mother is unmarried, and therefore not entitled to have any children on her permit. Sometimes it seems that even if they have the right documents, the authorities still order them out.

Some years ago, Alexandra Township, a black residential area nine miles outside Johannesburg, was gradually being cleared of its whole population preparatory to the bull-dozing of its houses and the building of barrack-hostels for 'single' men and 'single' women. Families that qualified for residence in Johannesburg under Section 10 were transferred to houses in the huge black township of Soweto, when houses were available. But a man who qualifies must have every person living with him in his house enumerated on his residential permit. Every man, woman or child must have his or her name on such a permit, or on a lodger's permit. Many men qualified, but their wives did not, and for the reasons given, many of the children were not registered. For months on end, police raided the houses, day and night. All those who lacked the necessary permits, tax receipts or papers were arrested; then the women, and their children, were 'endorsed out'. Sometimes women were arrested when their husbands were at work, or both husband and wife would be arrested. Then small children were left totally alone. Gradually the women were expelled to the reserves; those born in other places — Lesotho, or Swaziland — were expelled even if they had lived and worked a lifetime in South Africa.

When in 1972 the press published stories of children being left alone, or ordered away from their parents, Mr. Coen Kotze, who managed the local board dealing with Alexandra, stated that the women, if they were working, were given an alternative, "They are given ample time to make up their minds. We are giving them the choice: they must send their children back to the homelands themselves . . . This is the policy and we will enforce it." The children, he said, who were being ordered out were *illegal*; and their mothers were migrant workers recruited from the homelands on a single basis. "The law states that they are illegally in the area, so they have to go. It's as simple as that."(30)

The Black Sash magazine in June 1972 published the story of one of these women, Mrs. Masakona Molovhedzi, who went to the Black Sash Advice Office. She was a widow with three children, Eliza, Sarah and Selina, twelve, four and two years old, and she had been ordered to leave the prescribed area of Alexandra within 72 hours and to return to the Louis Trichardt area (some 400 miles to the north of Johannesburg) where she was born, but where she no longer had any relatives or friends. She had lived in Alexandra for more than 20 years, but she was unable to produce proof that would satisfy the authorities. Since her husband's death she had supported herself and her children by doing casual work.

She was sent to Nzhelele in the Louis Trichardt area, and the stark letters written to the Black Sash office tell how she arrived and was given a hut without a door and completely empty. "The welfare people sent me without a cent . . . no food to eat. My kids are hungry . . . I am trying to build a house." She asked for some money, and stamps so she could continue to write.

Two children became ill. There was no money to take them to a doctor. She received some money sent by the Black Sash, but none from a claim under the Workman's Compensation Fund concerning her husband's death. She bought a door for her hut and mealie meal (maize meal) and used the rest to pay for a journey to town to see the Bantu Affairs Commissioner. At the end of one letter was a postscript, which read: "N.B. The old lady Masakona is getting thin each day. I am writing this letter because I feel terrible about it. My name is Mr. Makaba Mphigalale. I always write her letters. Masakona is asking for soap to wash, could you phone the welfare? Please tell the welfare that Masakona is starving."

The next letter said: "The baby is so ill. Maybe the doctor at the hospital will admit her. I think the journey to town is too much for the kids. I have nobody to watch them when I am out."

Black women working as domestic servants for the whites in the towns are not permitted to have their babies or children living with them in their servants' rooms, which are usually in the yards of the white houses. Previously, white employers would often permit the servant to keep a baby, particularly when breast-fed, in her room, and the child would usually be sent away at three or four years. A new regulation prohibited this, and these babies and toddlers were also made 'illegal.'

Life in the hostels

In Cape Town less than 12,000 African families have any legal right to stay as family groups in the city's three townships. Of a total African population of over 110,000, about 56,000 are migrant contract workers living in hostels. The migrant workers constitute 85% of all African labour in the city. Men outnumber women by about 2.5:1, mainly because of the extent to which women have been endorsed out under the influx control legislation.

100,000 workers in Durban live their lives on a 'single person' basis, either in municipal hostels or in compounds built by private firms. Of these, about 30,000 are domestic servants housed in employers' backyards, but there are no figures here to show what proportion are women.

Johannesburg, with an acknowledged black population of 736,134 (this does not include the 367,000 men (migrants) housed in mine compounds), has the largest number of workers living in family houses in the vast township of Soweto — nearly 570,000 men, women and children. But in addition there are no less than 100,000 officially acknowledged migrant workers, the majority men, and the actual figure is much higher than this. [31]

It is nine miles outside Johannesburg, in what was Alexandra Township, that the most dramatic prototype of the new life planned for South Africa's blacks is

A call for volunteers during the Defiance Campaign, 1952

*Malnutrition and disease on a Natal farm.
(Photo by John Seymour)*

Ilinge, a resettlement area in the reserves. (Photo by John Seymour)

Family living conditions

Scene in Soweto. (*Photo by Abisag Tüllman*)

One third of women employed in S. Africa work as servants (Photo by Tony McGrath)

Citrus farm worker (Photo by Abisag Tüllman)

Demonstration by Trade Union organisers,
Rita Ndzanga and Mabel Balfour

Peasant women protest against the issuing of reference books (passes) to women.
Zeerust, Western Transvaal, 1957

Police baton charge spectators at a student demonstration, Johannesburg, 1972

Police attack women demonstrators at Cato Manor, Durban, 1959

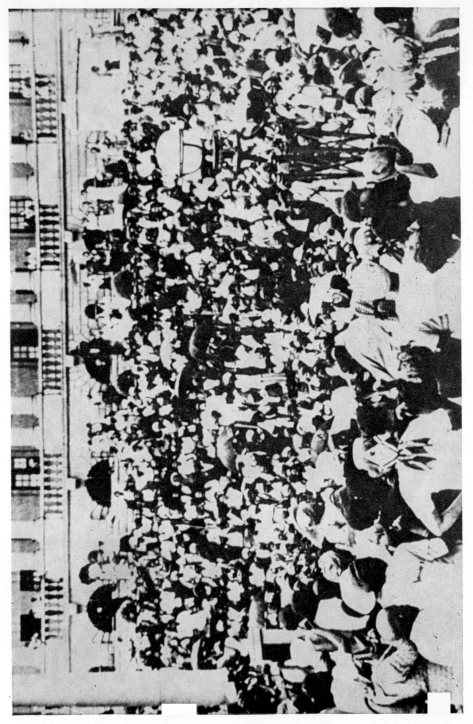

Mass demonstration of women against issue of passes to women, Pretoria, 1956

now arising. It is a new concept: a veritable city composed entirely of mammoth hostels, sex-separated. Eventually it is planned to house more than 60,000 single men and single women in this way, in 24 blocks.

Each hostel has a built-in police charge office; a thickly-walled cell; and a control room that operates electronic steel doors or riot gates that can block every passage in the hostel.

Through the one main entrance — a large, grilled gate — inmates' rooms open off endless corridors, mostly 4-bedded for women, and 4, 6 and 8-bedded for the men. Windows are six feet up, well above eye-level. There is no heating in the rooms, although Johannesburg winters are bitterly cold. All facilities are communal, with one washbasin for 11 inmates, 14 to a lavatory, 35 to a shower. In the kitchen, three people share a gas ring.

Members of the opposite sex, whether husbands or wives or not, may not be entertained in the rooms. No children are allowed. If children have to be brought to town for 'unavoidable' reasons (i.e. medical) they are not allowed to stay in the room with either parent, but may stay in the visitors' room for 10 cents a night. One woman's four-year-old child had to stay in the waiting room, crying bitterly, because her mother was not permitted to sleep with her own child, nor was the child allowed even to visit the mother's room or the kitchen. Women are locked up for the night in a punishment cell for the slightest offence.

Every inmate will bear the same number as her bed, her mattress and her locker. Living conditions are so minimal that they provide only the most basic of bare necessities — for example, there are 14 cubic metres of habitable space per person, the international minimum standard being 27 cubic metres. Yet the vast majority of migrant workers, and many who were not really migrant, will spend their lives in such conditions, for they have no hope of ever gaining permanent status in the white city, and there is no work for them in the Bantustans.

Their lives will be endless queues: in the mornings in corridors only four feet wide, queueing to wash; queueing to cook, to catch buses to work, to wash or iron clothes. Lack of privacy leads to depression, apathy, listlessness; and the conditions build tensions and frustrations that grossly affect the lives of the inmates, apart from the deviant behaviour and alcoholism that must be prevalent.

It is intended that recreational facilities (for tennis, soccer, swimming) will eventually be built round the hostels, and — on the women's side of the main street — churches.

How the system works

A. Mr. and Mrs. M. and their three children are typical of those forced apart. Although they each had a permit, the husband was working in Alexandra and the wife in Johannesburg, so they are not permitted to seek joint accommodation in another township. As he has not lived in Alexandra for 15 continuous years he does not qualify for a house. The husband is awaiting allocation of a bed in a hostel, the wife has been told to go to a hostel and that the children must be sent away. Where? To the homeland that is no homeland for they have never known it . . . to grandparents now dead . . . to strangers somewhere who might let them live in their own barren huts if the parents can send sufficient money . . . anywhere. Away. (*Black Sash, Feb.* 1973)

B. Mrs. Nxumalo was born in Alexandra and lived there all her life, and so have her children, who have birth certificates. But a few years ago she divorced her husband and moved to a new address, in her brother's house — but she was not enumerated on his housing permit. With some difficulty, she obtained a new permit to live in Alexandra but it was made out on a single basis for the duration of her employment only. It excluded her children. She has been told she must move into a hostel and that she should send her children to the homelands. (*Black Sash, Feb.* 1974)

C. Mrs. Opsie has no husband and lives with her only son, who is 16. She has been told to go to a woman's hostel and to put her son in a men's hostel. (*Black Sash, Feb.* 1974)

D. African women hired as servants in towns near Johannesburg are being made to sign away their children for as long as they work for whites. They have to pledge that they understand that they will lose their jobs if children or dependents join them on their employers' premises. Similarly, whites who employ African women as servants must sign a document that they will dismiss them if they bring children or dependents onto the premises. Documents are being issued to all African women from homeland areas who are allowed to work in the Johannesburg area on a 12-month contract. (*Daily Telegraph,* 21.9.73).

E. A 35-year-old African woman who had lived in the Cape for 30 years was fined R10 (or 30 days) for living illegally in the African township of Guguletu with her husband since 1968. She told the court she came to Cape Town in 1940, married in 1957, and lived in Nyanga East Township. In 1966, while she was away on a visit, her husband was transferred to the bachelor hostel at Guguletu. When she returned, she found a place to live there with him and their two children. (*Cape Times,* 5.12.70).

F. A crippled African factory worker of Wellington, Mr. Harlem Msini, was informed that his wife and 4-year-old child could not continue to live with him, after his wife had been convicted and fined R30 for being in an area illegally. Because she left the place where she was born, Dordrecht, and has forfeited her right to return, and because she has been endorsed out of the area where her husband lives, she is not legally entitled to live anywhere, and is a displaced person. Her case was taken up by the Black Sash, finally reaching the Deputy Minister of Bantu Administration, Dr. Koornhof, who rejected appeals saying there could be no condonation, as this would open the door to more such situations. "If all Bantu men are freely allowed to marry women who do not qualify . . . and are allowed to enter the territory, the numbers of Bantu will more than double." Subsequently, Mrs. Msini was given a temporary permit to live in Dordrecht, where she will live with her children, apart from her husband. (*Cape Times* 14.11.70-2.1.71).

G.   Mrs. Victoria Madi, 53, was born in Swaziland, but has lived in South Africa since 1936. She married in 1937 and has five children all born in South Africa. When her husband died, she was told she no longer qualified to remain in the urban area of Johannesburg and must return to the country of her origin — Swaziland. Mrs. Madi works in Johannesburg, all her children live in Johannesburg, where two are still at school, she has not been to Swaziland for 33 years and does not know anybody there. (*Rand Daily Mail* 3.11.69).

H.   A domestic servant, Mrs. Sara Makhomola, used to have her husband visit her and spend the night with her, as he worked only three miles away. This is illegal, but they were only caught twice. Now a new proclamation makes not only the Makhomolas, but also her white employer, liable to conviction and fine if her husband is caught sleeping with her. Their three children were sent to school in Pietersburg and now cannot visit their parents in Johannesburg without a permit. The family have no possible chance of living together. (*Rand Daily Mail* 21.3.70).

I.   Mrs. Bella Zwane, a widow, was deprived of her right to trade from her late husband's business. Her husband was formerly a grocer in Soweto, and under a government regulation a licence may be cancelled because of death. (No person can trade without a licence in the townships). The local African Chamber of Commerce organised a protest on Mrs. Zwane's behalf under the slogan 'isithukuthuku senja' — Zulu for 'sweat of a dog'. "We sweat for years to build shops in the hopes that these will support us and our children when we are gone. Then at the stroke of a pen, all is gone." (*Rand Daily Mail* 4.9.74).

J.   For 15 years Mr. Similo Mayor, a 48-year-old painter from Simonstown, has been trying to get a permit for his wife Manegela, whom he has seen for a total of less than four years in the 15 years they have been married, to stay with him in Cape Town. Mr. Mayor came to Cape Town in 1942 from his Transkei home near Tsomo. In 1951 he started work in the Naval dockyards, where he has been ever since. "I have no property or home in the Transkei. My wife must live with my brother in Tsomo. Our first five children went back to the Transkei with my wife. All of them died. The last three I have kept here in Cape Town, and they are alive but they have no mother." (*Cape Times* 30.11.74).

CHAPTER 7

Women at Work

For women everywhere the achievement of economic independence is a liberating force. Whatever else must still follow in obtaining access to higher levels of training and jobs, and in changing man's consciousness and their own status, it all starts with economic independence. When women become wage earners they are on the way to forcing open the doors to social, legal and political equality.

Ultimately African women too must achieve improved status from sustained economic growth. But not yet. While their economic role has declined within the framework of the old society, for the great majority there has been no opening of doors to compensating industrial employment. One reason is that South African industry has drawn on cheap labour reserves not only within its own borders, but from the whole under-developed sub-continent. Migrant labour from other countries releases local men to work on the farms, in the factories, and as domestic servants. Men are preferred for heavy manual labour, and — with a few exceptions, such as the food-canning industry in the Cape and the garment industry in the Transvaal — they are also employed in the light industrial work that in other countries is usually performed by women.

African women are however being more and more employed. The 1970 census showed that 25% of all African females were economically active, compared with 15% in 1960 and with roughly half of all African men (1970). As can be seen from the figures given in the Appendix (Table II), the majority of African women who work are employed either in service occupations (primarily as domestic servants) or in agriculture (as regular or casual farm labourers). In 1970 the former accounted for 38% and the latter for 35% of women in work. Only 4% of women workers are employed in manufacturing and transport, compared with 16% of African male workers.

The one-and-a-quarter million African women working in white households and farms are in fact occupied in extensions of their own traditional 'woman's role': cooking, cleaning, laundering, caring for children, cultivating. This is true in both the urban and rural areas. Women in the reserves who cultivate their own plots are classified as non-economically active 'housewives', and there are few other employment opportunities. The figures given for employment in the Bantu Homelands (see Table III) show that only some 17% of the total female population of the reserves was employed in 1970, and of those who were, the overwhelming majority (80%) worked either as farm labourers or domestic servants. The numbers employed in the professions open to African women, teaching and nursing, are extremely small (some 4% of women workers in the reserves), and other jobs are virtually non-existent.

The same applies in the 'white' rural areas, where 28% of the African female population of these areas are employed, and again the vast majority of these (85%) work on white farms and households.

In the towns there are more job opportunities for black women. In South Africa the rise of industry was characterised in the first place by the development of heavy industry — that is mining — which up to the time of the second world war remained by far and away the largest factor in industrial life. Since mining demands male labour, black women have not (and are only now to a limited extent) been drawn into industrial production in the same numbers as working women were in other countries during their periods of rapid industrialisation. In the countryside the women carried on their heavy manual load of labour in the fields and in the preparation of food and care of the children; in the towns the only avenues opened to them were again the continuation of domesticity outside the home: as domestic servants in the homes of the whites; or, for a lucky few, in nursing and teaching, again an extension of their 'woman's' role.

Of the total female population in the 'white' urban areas, a much higher proportion (37%) are in paid employment (partly of course as a result of the removal of non-productive Africans from the urban areas). However, the majority of these (65%) are again servants, followed by smaller proportions of manufacturing (8%) and professional (7%) workers.

Domestic service is therefore the main occupation of African women in both town and country. Other working women are employed in occupations also connected with household needs, in food processing or canning works, in garment manufacturing and laundering, and in teaching and nursing. In general, however, African women are excluded from two other jobs commonly filled by women elsewhere — clerical workers and shop assistants — and from a whole range of professional occupations, as well as from skilled trades and other industrial occupations. The public services, banks, building societies, mining houses and other corporations employ a large number of women in administrative and secretarial jobs, but nearly all of them are white. While a secretarial shortage in recent years has led to the training of some Coloured and African girls as typists, telephonists etc, black office workers are seldom acceptable to their white colleagues.

The double discrimination of race and sex excludes African women from many professions (see Table IV). By 1973 there were no African women lawyers, judges, magistrates, engineers, architects, veterinary surgeons, chemists or pharmacists. African women doctors, university teachers and librarians were a rarity. Only in school teaching and nursing are there more African women than men (and roughly the same numbers as white women, from a larger population).

In general Africans are not apprenticed to skilled trades, but men can qualify as building and mining artisan's assistants, electric wiremen, woodworkers and surveyor assistants, which women may not do. Of the small numbers of Africans admitted to technical or vocational training, girls are far outnumbered by boys, and undertake mainly courses in dressmaking, home management, health care and so on.

Where women are employed in industry or in the professions, their wages are always lower than those of men doing the same work, or of whites doing the same type of work. African teachers, for instance, do not have equal pay, and in 1974 the salary scales for men with identical qualifications were some R170-740 higher than those for women (see Table V). Such discrimination appears at all levels of the education system and in all branches of the public service open to Africans.

Moreover African women at the black university colleges and in the public service who marry have their jobs terminated by law — this, of course, does not apply to male employees.

At the other end of the social scale, even the payments ('gratuities') made to prisoners for various kinds of work done under prison regulations discriminate not only among the races, but also between men and women, with female African prisoners receiving the minimum.

In secondary industry, African women are slowly making headway, starting at the bottom of the ladder in jobs for which men are considered less suitable or too expensive. They also find a foothold in those industries for which white or Coloured women are not available, usually in the lowest-paid jobs.

The pattern of women's employment is undergoing change and there are exceptions to the general picture. In the clothing industry on the Witwatersrand, for instance, African women work as fully qualified machinists. As wages go, they are relatively well paid, but here too they are paid less than men; the basic weekly wage for textile workers in the main urban areas in 1975 was fixed at R15 (£9) for men and R12 (£7.50) for women (see Table VI). In the border areas the basic female rate was R9.60 (£6).

"African women want paid employment. There are no conventions and traditional taboos that restrain them from working outside the home. Illiteracy and inadequate schooling are obstacles, but hardly more so for them than for the men. Almost as many girls as boys attend primary and secondary schools. The elimination rate is high. Fewer than 1,000 wrote the matriculation examination in 1962 and only 40% of the candidates passed. More boys than girls matriculate, but the general level of education is much the same for both sexes. Under-employment among African women is a result of land hunger, insufficient utilization of human and natural resources, and discrimination against women on grounds of both sex and race."[32]

Despite their relative under-representation in industrial occupations, where they are employed in industry, black women have been active and prominent in the field of labour organisation and the trade union movement. This is particularly true of the garment and textile industries, and food canning and processing, where the majority of workers are women.

Historically, the leading role taken by women in union organisation was facilitated by the fact that the main law covering labour organisation, the

Industrial Conciliation Act, excluded "pass bearing natives" from its provisions. Until women were forced to carry passes this enabled them to take an active role in the formation of trade unions, particularly in the 1940s and 50s. African trade unions had no status but many black women gained invaluable experience. Among Coloured workers, whose unions were recognised, several women became the best known and most militant of the workers' spokesmen.

Despite governmental opposition to black labour organisation and the many difficulties put in their way, black women in manufacturing courageously continue to organise; their sisters in domestic and farm service, however, remain totally unrepresented.

CHAPTER 8

Women in the Political Struggle
Makabongwe Amakosikazi

Just as it is not possible to discuss the problems and disabilities of South African women without discussing the problems and disabilities that apartheid inflicts on the whole black population, so also it is not possible to assess the women's political activities and struggles without surveying the general struggle for liberation.

Women know that simply to fight for some improved status or rights within the framework of the apartheid state is all but useless. The changes that are needed are over-riding: black women need the right to vote, as black men also need. Without political power there is little hope of changing their own immediate problems of jobs, homes, education.

The severest disabilities afflicting the women of South Africa are those arising from the racist society. However, in their activities the women have brought into play certain characteristics which are peculiarly theirs.

Despite their background of a patriarchal tribal society, African women have never occupied the positions of absolute subservience that still exist in some parts of Asia and Africa. Even before the tribal pattern had been shattered as it is today, the women played a notable part in many political struggles. On the whole, women have participated in the general struggle for liberation together with the men, and in tracing women's political activities it is not possible to separate these from the aims of the struggles for national liberation as a whole, nor from the inummerable campaigns in which women and men participated together.

In these campaigns, although a significant number of women played increasingly important parts, the leadership as a whole was usually male-dominated, but certainly not more so than we find in countries like England where women have had a much longer tradition of political struggle.

Boycotts

The war years brought dramatic industrial growth to South Africa, accelerating the steady shift of population from country to town. Industry was a magnet pulling peasants from the stagnating reserves, and as the laws at that time did not prohibit the women from entering the urban areas a large number of black workers settled with their families on the fringes of the industrial areas. The growth of industry was totally dependent on this great pool of labour, but their housing and other needs were totally neglected by local and government authorities alike.

The pressures were particularly sharp in Johannesburg. In 1943, 15,000 men and women walked 18 miles a day for nine days in protest against a 1d. rise in bus fares. They lived in Alexandra Township, nine miles outside Johannesburg, and worked in the city. In mid-winter, in the sharp cold of the high-veld, domestic servants and washerwomen carrying grotesque loads of clothes on their heads, marched together with factory and shop workers from early morning when it was still dark until late at night. A year later there was a second boycott, this time lasting seven weeks. Many middle-class white women drove their cars to and from Alexandra morning and evening specifically to give lifts to women, particularly the older women who found the long walk most exhausting.

The drivers were stopped by the police, who charged them with carrying passengers without a permit. These white women encountered for the first time in their lives the sharp edge of opposition to authority, and the abysmal poverty and hardship of the lives of the black women.

The huge influx into black townships reached bursting point in 1944 when, in the words of one of their leaders, "the people overflowed". A series of squatters movements began in which families who had been living as sub-tenants in small houses already overcrowded, set up their own shanty towns on the hillsides surrounding Johannesburg. The women played an essential part in the long conflicts with municipal and government authorities and as always their burden was greater because on them fell the major share of the physical work and hardships of life in homes made of sacking and cardboard.

Indian women were among 600 Indians in Natal jailed for a campaign of passive resistance to a new segregation act which they called the Ghetto Act. The campaign was also the beginning of a new unity of action between the African National Congress and the Indian Congress.

In 1949, following the return of a Nationalist Government in the (whites only) general election, the African National Congress benefitting from a new dynamism coming from its Youth League, adopted a new Programme of Action calling for 'strikes, civil disobedience and non-cooperation'. As a first step a one-day stoppage of work was called for May 1st. Police fired into crowds of people in the townships, killing 18 and wounding 30, including children. The outburst of sorrow and anger that followed the shootings brought together the African National Congress, the Indian Congress and the Communist Party (then about to be declared illegal) in a committee formed to call a national stoppage of work as protest on June 26th, 1950. Hundreds of thousands took part in what was primarily a protest against apartheid; schools were empty, shops in the townships and particularly Indian shops in Johannesburg and Durban were closed. In Port Elizabeth the stoppage was spectacular — all shipping was halted, businesses closed, and hotels and garages were left without staff.

(Because all strikes of Africans are illegal, the term 'general strike' was not used, as this would lay all those organising it open to arrest. Hence the 'stoppage'

— later to become the 'stay-at-home' — was the form adopted.)
From that time on, June 26th became Freedom Day for South Africa.

Defiance Campaign

The 1950's were the turbulent years of political activity, beginning with the African National Congress conference of 1951 which approved a non-violent campaign to coincide with 6th April 1952 which was being celebrated by whites as Van Riebeeck Day — the day 300 years before when whites first landed in the Cape. During this whole decade, up to 1960, the emphasis of all the campaigns was on peaceful protest, on non-violent methods of struggle. The campaign launched, that of Defiance against Unjust Laws, marked a peak in mass action together with discipline, humour, and good-nature on the part of the participants. 8,500 people deliberately courted arrest by defying apartheid regulations and laws, and among those who went to jail was a fair proportion of women. Africans, Indians and whites, together with an organisation of the Coloured people, all participated in the campaign.

The liberation movement, now broad-based, having achieved unity between the different races, proved itself capable of sophisticated campaigns. It had acquired symbols — a flag, a national anthem, a salute. The women wore a uniform — the black and green blouses that symbolised support for the African National Congress. The Freedom songs composed for each new activity were sung throughout the country.

But each new protest was met by counter-action by the government in the form of new laws that effectively prevented similar protests in the future. The Defiance Campaign brought the Public Safety Act, empowering the government to call a state of emergency, and the Criminal Laws Amendment Act, with prison, lashes and fines for anyone supporting the commission of an offence in protest against any laws, and preventing the collection of monies for such protest campaigns. Prohibitions and banning orders began to cripple the organisations.

The huge Congress of the People in June 1955 drew up a Freedom Charter for all South Africans, and in addition to new oppressive laws, brought the arrest of 156 men and women of all races on charges of treason. The 4½-year-long trial ended in the acquittal of all the accused, but together with increased bannings and Security Police action it helped to slow down the whole protest movement. In 1957 and 1958 there were widespread revolts in many country areas (including those involving the women's anti-pass campaigns) that were met with excessive cruelty, assaults on people, and burning of their homes and possessions. 26 June 1957 was the start of a campaign of boycott — this, too, became illegal soon afterwards — and the tightening network of new laws and police activity brought ever-increasing repression and brutality.

21 March 1960 was the date of one of the most horrifying examples of this. The Pan-Africanist Congress, founded in 1958, called a demonstration against the pass laws at Sharpeville. Faced with a large peaceful crowd of protest, the police opened fire. In a bloody scene 69 men and women were killed and 180 wounded.

42

This atrocity was followed by the declaration of a State of Emergency lasting five months. Raids and detentions were on a mass scale. Twenty white women were among the large number of African, Coloured, Indian and white men and women who were detained, an indication of the solidarity forged between the different racial elements during the years of activity although the bulk of those detained were of course African. Terror became the rule.

The African National Congress and the Pan-Africanist Congress were banned. The last legal action taken was the calling of a National Convention by black leaders for May 1961. On the very day when the white electorate went to vote the Nationalist government in for a new 5-year term of office, eight leading Africans were sentenced to a year in jail for advocating one man, one vote.

The general strike called for 29th May 1961, brought army mobilisation, helicopters and tanks in the townships, and the largest display of naked force brought into play to crush this last, theoretically legal, demonstration against apartheid laws. It was a climax and turning point in political struggle in South Africa. Seven months later the first acts of sabotage took place, with the emergence of Umkhonto we Sizwe, the military wing of the now illegal ANC.

Indefinite detention without trial, solitary confinement and torture brought in an era of political trials. The women now had to shoulder enormous burdens.

Women's resistance

Throughout the long years of resistance women have played an important part alongside the men. In addition they have initiated and sustained their own protests against the apartheid system, demonstrating a strength which is wonderful when one considers both their greater insecurity and oppression and their responsibilities — often carried singlehandedly — for homes and children.

A Women's League attached to the African National Congress of South Africa remained for many years a means of organising women for the national liberation struggle, but also served as a means of obtaining the usual work out of the women — feeding and finding accommodation for delegates to conferences, and similar work. In the liberation movement individual women have played outstanding roles as organisers, speakers, leaders: but, as in other countries, proportionately their numbers have been much smaller than the men, and they were scarcely to be seen at top leadership levels.

Because of their comparatively small numbers in industry, black women in general lack the experience in work-solidarity relationships that have often provided a training ground for male political leaders. Domestic servants cannot join together to ask for high wages or better conditions; each has, individually, to deal with an individual employer.

Despite these handicaps, when they have been roused to action the women have displayed qualities over and above those of the men: a courage as great, often greater because of the immediate responsibility for the children at home; a longer, stronger tenacity, as though the women felt that once they had taken a difficult decision to embark on perilous action, it could not be abandoned; and over and above all else something totally South African — a transfiguring gaiety, a sense of fun, a most joyful spirit that illuminated conferences, strikes, meetings, and turned even mass arrests into a kind of holiday. Domestic servants, climbing into the police pick-up vans after being arrested for protesting against the pass laws, cried out gaily to spectators: "Tell our Madams we won't be at work today!"

The women were always singing. When the Women's Federation held conferences in a hall in Johannesburg, the contingents of women arriving from different areas could be heard down the street, singing as they marched to the hall, the music sounding louder and louder until, as they entered the hall, those already there rose to their feet and a great tide of thrilling and beautiful sound swelled out into the quiet Sunday streets in matchless harmony. It always held up the proceedings, especially as many contingents, handicapped by long distances and poor transport, came late. But it brought to the assembled women a sense of joy and of power, and an amity that carried over into their political deliberations.

The beautiful voice of one of the women leaders, Ida Mtwana of the Transvaal ANC Women's League, can never be forgotten. Her powerful voice poured out freedom songs as police smashed up meetings, restoring calm and renewing the peoples' determination. Her voice, her strength and calm courage were a rallying point that brought strength to others and embodied hope, yearning, determination.

The people composed new songs for every occasion. There was a song about Bantu Education, one commemorating a leader's visit abroad, and one, mourning the banning of a leader, which was adapted to each new victim in turn. Songs marked the Defiance Campaign, the potato boycott, the Congress of the People. Songs celebrated the pick-up vans and the women's campaign against passes.

In jail the women sang hymns on Sundays, and in 1960 when the jails were filled with political prisoners, freedom songs alternated with the hymns. That has passed now. In Barberton jail where women political prisoners serve their sentences, singing of any kind is prohibited, even the singing of hymns on Sundays.

Police who arrived in a country village to arrest about 20 women who had burned their pass-books, found 200 women patiently sitting together under the trees.[33] The sergeant demanded the women for whom he had come. "We are here", the women replied.

He asked them to step forward. "If you arrest one, you must arrest us all", they said.

The sergeant had to hire railway buses to transport the women to jail; their number had increased to 233. They filled the yard of the police station — singing. Food had to be provided; the jail could not cope with them, nor the sanitation. When they were told they were being released, the women demanded buses to take them home. The crowd of arrested women had unaccountably increased from 233 to 400.

44

The women formed a procession around the sergeant and his aides, singing a new song with many verses, and the refrain:

> Behold us joyful,
> The women of Africa,
> In the presence of our *baas*:
> The great one
> Who conquers Lefurutse
> With his knobkerrie,
> And his assagai,
> And his gun.

Pass Campaign

The most prolonged struggle by women of South Africa centred around their refusal to accept passes. Until the 1950's passes had to be carried only by African men.

The operation of the pass laws is an essential part of the control of the migratory labour and the flow of workers to the towns. In certain periods, because of the relative insignificance of female wage labour, African women were not subject to the same controls. The pass laws and numerous other laws and regulations controlling residence, movement and conditions of work, have been extended to women only during the past two decades, with the intention of using them as a means to force all women and children not required as domestic servants in the towns to live in the reserves.

The women's struggle against passes and permits began as long ago as 1913 in the Orange Free State. Women who lived in the urban locations were forced to buy a new permit each month that cost them a shilling (at a time when £2 a month was an excellent wage). When petitions and deputations had failed, the women "threw off their shawls and took the law into their own hands".[34] In Bloemfontein 600 women marched to the municipal offices and demanded to see the Mayor. When they were told he was out, they deposited a bag containing their passes at the feet of the Deputy-Mayor and told him they would buy no more.

Similar demonstrations spread to other towns and many women were arrested and sentenced to various terms of imprisonment. If they were given the option of a fine, they all refused to pay, and at small country jails officials were confronted with the problem of a mass of women prisoners for whom they were not equipped.

Singing hymns, 800 women marched from the location to the Town Hall in the Free State town of Winburg, and told the authorities they were tired of making appeals that bore no fruit, and thus they had resolved to carry no more passes. In a tiny Free State *dorp* this mass demonstration of women was a stupendous event and made a striking impression. But the authorities were adamant and continued to arrest women, who had to be carted from one small town to another to find sufficient jail accommodation.

The struggle continued for years, and eventually these dauntless women were successful. Passes for women were withdrawn.

In 1955 the then Minister of Native Affairs stated "African women will be issued with passes as from January 1956". In fact the law had been amended in 1950 to enable the Government to introduce passes for women.

Women had reason to fear the carrying of passes, having been forced to witness all their lives the effect of the pass laws on African men: the night raids, stopping in streets by police vans, searches, jobs lost through arrests, disappearance of men shanghaied to farms, and the prosecutions (nearly 700,000 in 1968). It was not even known at the time the degree to which the pass laws would be used to separate family groups and break up homes. But women did know the devastating effect the laws could have on some aspects of their lives. For the men, arrest for pass offences could mean loss of job; but for women? They might or might not have a job to lose, but most of them had helpless dependents, often very young babies, who could not be left totally unattended when the mother was whisked off the streets and into jail.

The first big protest against the pass laws took place in October 1955 with 2,000 women, mostly Africans, but including women of all the other races, converging in Pretoria, seat of the administration of the Government. The demonstration had been a response to one organised many months before by the Black Sash, white women protesting against pass laws. The black women said, "The white women did not invite us to their demonstration, but we will invite all women, no matter what race or colour".

The women's anti-pass movement began to grow. In Durban and Cape Town women marched in their thousands through the streets. The men were amazed at their independence and militancy, but Lilian Ngoyi, African women's leader, explained: "Men are born into the system and it is as if it has become a life tradition that they carry passes. We as women have seen the treatment our men have — when they leave home in the morning you are not sure if they will come back. If the husband is to be arrested, *and* the mother, what about the child?"(35)

The government began the issue of passes by selecting sections of the women least likely or able to protest: farmers brought lorry-loads of women workers from their farms to get their passes and the women knew what would happen if they refused. Even these country women would sometimes subsequently burn their passes and protests grew all over the country, culminating in a mass demonstration in Pretoria, one year after the first one, on 9 August 1956 — the day that has since been designated "Women's Day" in South Africa.

A year before it had been 2,000 women. Now 20,000 women assembled, overcoming tremendous difficulties imposed both by their personal positions and by the authorities, to join the assembly. Despite the most ingenious forms of intimidation the women saved and worked together to raise money to hire trains, buses, cars, to bring them thousands of miles to the capital. All processions in Pretoria were banned that day, so the women walked to Union Buildings to see the Prime Minister in groups of never more than three. All Pretoria was filled with women. This was four years before the national liberation organisations were banned, and thousands of women wore the green and black Congress blouses; Indian women dressed in brilliant saris; Xhosa women in their ochre robes with elaborate headscarves.

Union Buildings is designed in classic style, with pillared wings on either side of an amphitheatre on a hillside, with trees and gardens in steps down the hillside and a vista to the town far down below across a long avenue of lawn. The women slowly converged up this avenue and filled the amphitheatre. Their leaders went into Union Buildings and left hundreds of thousands of signatures on petition forms at the office of the Prime Minister who, of course, was not available to see them. Afterwards they stood in complete silence in the winter sun — even the babies on their backs did not cry — for thirty minutes, then burst into magnificent harmony to sing the anthems, *Nkosi sikile'i Afrika* and *Morena Boloka*. The singing, as they dispersed, echoed over the city, and the women began a new freedom song with its refrain "Wathint' a bafazi, way ithint' imbolodo uzo kufa" — Now you have touched the women you have struck a rock, you have dislodged a boulder, you will be crushed.

The protests continued, but so did the issue of passes. The authorities made it inevitable; old women who went to collect their tiny pensions were told "No pass book — no pension". Mothers could not obtain the registration of the birth of a child unless they had their passbook. Teachers and nurses were dismissed if they refused to take passes. Gradually more and more women were forced to accept them.

Not only did the more sophisticated women of the towns organise in protest. Remote country districts were involved, and the struggle was most bitter in the area of Zeerust, in the Western Transvaal. The movement was an instinctive response of the women, mothers and growers of crops, to protect their children and their homes. They resisted. In one village, only 76 out of 4,000 women accepted books, and many later burned them. A local chief sympathised with the women, and he was arbitrarily removed, a Government appointee put in his place, with a gang of strongarm thugs. The revolt against passes spread to become resistance to the stooge chiefs and the new laws under Bantu authorities.

Under the direction of a gross and sadistic police sergeant, Van Rooyen, a terrible punishment was exacted from the people. Many were shot, more beaten, their homes burned to the ground and all their possessions destroyed, and then the people became dispersed, individuals were sent into banishment, others had to hide for months on end.

"The women in the first group were slashed raw. They said that 23 other women were similarly injured 'but we do not know where they have run'. Injuries were distributed mainly about their arms, backs and shoulders, but their faces, breasts and bellies and thighs had suffered too. The standard injury was a sort of gash of varied length. Clothes clotted with blood adhered to the wounds . . .".[36] The wounds had been inflicted by bodyguards of the government's stooge-chiefs, with strips cut from tyres and sharpened at one side like a knife.

Mrs. Makgoro Maletsoe, who burned her pass book, was sent to jail and on release crept quietly back to her village at Witkleigat. She knew the chief's thugs were beating up those who had resisted the pass laws. On her return, she saw another group of women being arrested, and among them a friend who she knew had an unweaned infant. Makgoro Maletsoe ran to her friend's hut and fetched the baby, which she handed to its mother before she was taken away. This roused the bodyguard who surrounded the women and then attacked them with clubs and kieries. The group were then cast into a hut where they spent the night, "Mrs. Maletsoe hovering between an agonizing wakefulness and insensibility. She had entirely lost the use of her right arm, and her face and body were smashed and torn."

These women were not charged with any crime. The next morning the regular police came, brandishing guns, but eventually set them free. "By devious routes, despairing friends managed to get Makgoro Maletsoe out of the sprawling village, into a car, and away to Johannesburg . . . for a month she lay in a hospital bed. Besides the injuries inflicted on her face and torso by boots and kieries, her right arm was broken in three places." When she was well enough, she laid a charge of assault. The Attorney-General declined to prosecute.

This was the price of political struggle for women in South Africa.

Women were in the lead, also, in Cato Manor in Durban, in protests that arose in the first place from extreme poverty. In the Cato Manor shack settlement women complained that their husbands' wages were grossly inadequate and that the administration provided no lights and no sewerage; they complained about nightly police raids, a constant invasion of their homes. The women and children held a protest, and when this was ignored, the women's anger began to centre on grievances arising from the system of municipal beer halls. Throughout the country, for thirty years, there had been deep resentment that the law prevented Africans from brewing traditional beer, which in turn warped customs of traditional hospitality. The men could go to municipal beer halls to drink. The women argued the halls should be closed and they should be allowed to brew. The discontent at Cato Manor exploded in June 1959, when 2,000 women gathered to tell their grievances to a local official; and the police, loathed both for their personal behaviour and as instruments of oppressive laws, charged the women with batons, striking the women on the ground, often hitting the babies tied to their backs.

There were riots and seething discontent spread to the Natal countryside. The boycott of beer halls became the focus of discontent, with women picketing them in a number of municipalities. The response of the authorities was to intensify police action against illegal brewing.

In rural areas the frustration and anger focused on the dipping tanks for cattle which women were forced to maintain by unpaid labour. Sometimes the protests were peaceful, sometimes violent. Many dipping tanks were destroyed; and where police baton-charged women pickets outside the beer halls, the people retaliated by burning Bantu Education schools.

48

The protests set up a chain reaction, and the upheavals went on. Hundreds of women were arrested and jailed — in one village a jail built for 115 prisoners had 482. Police trying to disperse a crowd of women found them kneeling and praying in front of them. The police arrested the entire crowd — nearly 400 women — who were fined £35 or four months imprisonment. None paid the fines. Through the many mass trials, the spirit of the women of Natal remained uncrushed.

In September 1959 when the African National Congress convened a special conference, a bright red banner proclaimed MAKABONGWE AMAKOSI-KAZI — we thank the women.

CHAPTER 9

The Struggle Continues

When the harsh anti-terrorism legislation was introduced in the early 1960s women were among those who suffered the solitary confinement, indefinite detention without trial and torture that accompanied it. Some were involved directly in the arrests and political trials; others were affected through the long and often uncertain imprisonment of husbands, fathers, sons and friends.

Women were prosecuted on a wide variety of political charges including treason, terrorism, sabotage, membership of or assistance to a banned organisation, helping people to escape from the country, recruiting guerillas, breaches of banning orders and similar charges. Among those who have served jail sentences are women of all colours and all ages and religions. There have been young girls, many mothers, and grandmothers, some over 70.

Under South African security legislation, political activists who do not heed police warnings are subject to a variety of punishments, for actions which, insofar as they relate to demands for equal political and civil rights, cannot be considered crimes. They may be detained indefinitely without trial, interrogated and often tortured; they may be prosecuted and imprisoned, without remission or parole, for contravening political 'laws'; and they may be served with restriction ('banning') and/or house arrest orders, when manifold curbs are placed on movement, political activity, employment and social life for a period of up to five years, renewable.

Women have been among the many to suffer these forms of political persecution. In the early 1960s, scores of women were detained, often for lengthy periods. Over 200 were brought to trial, of whom 83 served prison sentences. Some 150 women have been subject to banning and house arrest orders; at the end of 1977 there were 30 women under banning orders, some for the third time.

The early 1960s were years of widespread political trials as the police clamped down on all forms of political organisation. In 1963 two young African women, Cynthia Lichaba and Patricia Pethala were found guilty of belonging to the banned PAC and furthering its aims by carrying letters. Both were sentenced to 18 months imprisonment.

In 1963 four women — all teachers — were among the 11 people convicted of sabotage and of belonging to the National Liberation Front, and imprisoned. Dulcie September, Dorothy Alexander and Doris van der Heyden were sentenced to 5 years and Elizabeth van der Heyden to 10 years. Although the sentences were imposed under the Sabotage Act, no evidence of sabotage acts was presented; the accused were convicted of conspiracy on the grounds that they read and studied the works of Lenin and Mao. On release all were banned and restricted for a further five years.

Women were also not spared the torture of prolonged solitary confinement and of physical assault. Many women, white and black, endured the agony of 'statue' torture, forced to stand continuously day and night without rest or sleep until they reached a state of mental disorientation and physical collapse.

Mrs. Rita Ndzanga was one of 17 men and 5 women who were victims of a prolonged police operation of arrest, detention without trial, charges and trial and discharge, and then re-arrest. Her husband was arrested in the same series of trials, and they had four young children who were left to be cared for by friends.

"My first interrogation took place on 16th May, I was taken to a room at the back of Compol Buildings. Major Swanepoel called me by my name. I kept quiet and did not reply. Other Security Police continued to question me. Day and night is the same in this room because of the thick heavy planks covering the windows.

"I remained standing. It was late at night. One policeman came round the table towards me and struck me. I fell to the floor. He said 'Staan op!' and kicked me while I lay on the floor."

They poured water on her face. A new team of interrogators came in and told her she would be kept standing until she spoke. During the third period of interrogation they began hitting her, then made her take off her shoes and stand on some bricks. One of the Security Police climbed a chair and pulled her by her hair, dropping her on the bricks. They did this again and again each time she fell. "The man who pulled me by the hair had his hands full of my hair." At last she managed to stand up, and they said 'On the bricks!' and hit her when she fell.(37)

Late in 1976 Rita and Lawrence Ndzanga were again detained. Lawrence died at the hands of the security police interrogators. Rita was released, but not until the day after the funeral.

Shantie Naidoo was held in solitary confinement by the police with the intention that she should appear as a witness against her friends and comrades on trial. When she was called to give evidence she refused, saying that she could not live with her conscience if she did. The judge told her she would go to prison for two months and would be called again, and if she still refused to give evidence she would go back to jail. "I am prepared to accept it," she said.

Then she told the court how she had been in solitary confinement for six months, sleeping on the floor of her cell, often going without any exercise for days or weeks.

She gave the most graphic account any court had yet heard of the effects of interrogation coupled with prolonged sleeplessness. She stood for five days and five nights, interrogated all the time. "I lost track of time and for periods my mind went blank." At one stage, after such a blackout, she dreamed she was being interrogated, and spoke to the interrogation officer in her sleep.

Another woman called as witness, Brysine Mamkahla, also refused to give evidence and was sent back to jail.[38]

Sometimes women were jailed simply because of their husband's political activities. Lettie Sibeko was arrested because Security Police wanted her husband, and could not find him. She was two months pregnant when she was arrested, and she was released without charge just before her baby was born, after seven months solitary confinement in a cell without bed or chair. Caroline Motsoaledi, mother of seven children of whom the youngest was a breast-fed baby of two months, was arrested during the trial of her husband Elias and held for five months in solitary confinement under the iniquitous 90-days law. When she was eventually released her husband had been sentenced to life imprisonment and taken a thousand miles away to Robben Island. A white woman, Pixie Benjamin, the mother of three small children, went on a hunger-strike lasting 48 days in protest against her arrest and detention without trial. The wife of another political prisoner, was in court when her husband, Michael Ngubeni, was sentenced to twelve years imprisonment for attempted sabotage (a police agent had organised the whole affair). When Ngubeni was sentenced she cried out as her husband was taken away: "I'm proud of you, my husband! Twelve years — it's nothing!"

The names of these women are mentioned here not because they are unique, but because they are typical of the reaction of South African women to the intense persecution which began in the 1960's.

Scarcely less than political activity, trade union activity by the black people has been regarded with disfavour by the Nationalist government — since it threatens the basis of cheap labour on which apartheid is built. And ever since women began to play an important part in union activity they, like the men, have suffered the various penalties devised by the apartheid state.

Liz Abrahams, for instance, in the Food and Canning Workers Union, has an impressive record of achieving higher wages and better working conditions for the workers in that industry, the majority of whom are women. For her activities she was banned — silenced and excluded from the trade union movement. Other well known black trade unionists are Mary Moodley, Rita Ndzanga, Mabel Balfour and Viola Hashe. Mention must also be made of the white women who were prominent in organising workers across the colour-line — Ray Alexander and Betty du Toit being the most outstanding of these. All these too have been banned, detained or imprisoned for their activities.

The Dependents

At the height of the political arrests and trials it was estimated that there were forty to fifty thousand dependents of political prisoners. In 1964 a Port Elizabeth newspaper carried the following report:

"The most touching aspect of the arrest of three hundred-odd Africans on political charges in the Port Elizabeth area is the great distress and hardship suffered by the mothers and close on 1,000 children. As most of these political widows and orphans trudge up and down the city and townships, seeking shelter, food, clothes, medical care and comfort, they wonder at the lack of sympathy and response. The disappearance of their husbands seems to have brought them to the end of the world. Many mothers have no less than 5 minor children, and some have 7 or 9. Some children have nobody to look after them. They fend for themselves. In one home, the young woman was arrested last year; her small children aged 2, 3 and 4 years remained in the custody of her mother. The old woman had to care for her own five children and the three grandchildren.

"Then the worst happened. The old woman was arrested. All her children and the three grandchildren were stranded; the 17-year-old daughter had to take charge of the family, without money . . .

"Four children have been without their mother for more than a year. She was arrested, and then after many months, charged; then released, then re-arrested..."

Another journalist wrote of 21-year-old Josie Nonyaniso who was left to look after five small brothers and sisters when her parents were jailed, her father for eight years and her mother for $4\frac{1}{2}$ years. Josie's own husband died, and she had a baby of her own to care for as well. There was also Mrs Philomen Khunge who alone had to care for 11 children. Her mother (sentenced to $4\frac{1}{2}$ years) left her with nine; her husband (nine years in jail) left her with two. The only sister who might have been able to help was also in jail for being a member of the African National Congress.

"The catalogue of hardships, even among people accustomed to hardship, is long. And the tales of tragedy are frequent, such as the one Grandfather Mali told. His son, Freddie, had been sentenced to eight years in November, and Freddie's wife to seven years the following April. They had four children aged 11, 9, 7 and 3, whom the grandparents took into their own home. But the cost of supporting the children proved too heavy and when they fell behind with their rent they were evicted from their home, they had to send the children away to relatives. Soon after the youngest fell ill and died."[39]

At that time the humanitarian Defence and Aid Fund assisted the families of political prisoners, and provided money for the baby's funeral. But not long after the government banned the South African Defence and Aid Fund. Nevertheless its work has been maintained by the International Defence and Aid Fund.

In theory, once a man is convicted and sent to prison, his family is eligible for State assistance at the rate of £1.10 a month. In practice even this miserable amount is hardly ever paid, and in many cases families are too frightened to approach the authorities. The conviction and imprisonment of the man often leads to the endorsing out of his family who lose the right to live in the townships and are sent to resettlement camps.

Thus the participation of the women in the political struggle in South Africa is not confined simply to those who are directly involved, but spreads to encompass wives, mothers and grandmothers throughout the country. Often they are left alone to contend with all the problems of poverty, work and child-rearing together with the additional problems of homelessness, expulsion to the reserves and all the hideous distortions of life that these impose.

It takes courage, in South Africa, to speak out against oppression, courage and endurance too. Wives have seen their husbands arrested and imprisoned; mothers, particularly since the Soweto shootings of 1976, have seen their children disappear, often not knowing if they have been killed by the police, taken into detention, or forced into exile. The burden is heavy.

Women in Resistance

Because the women's struggle has always been an integral part of the whole struggle against apartheid, the overt signs of activity within South Africa have only appeared from time to time. With the end in 1961 of the long era of non-violent activities, the women, and their former organisations, became part of the underground resistance and the general preparations for armed struggle to end apartheid.

While it was still possible for organisations to operate legally, the influence of the women in national liberation organisations had begun to grow, and their participation at all levels had become more and more important. The Women's League of the ANC was no longer simply fulfilling the role of background support for the activities more usually organised by men; and individual women were achieving positions of importance and influence. While there is obviously a need — as in every country throughout the world — for a change in male consciousness and re-assessment of what have always been considered the traditional male and female roles, it must be said that on the whole where women within the political movement have taken up positions of leadership, these are generally accepted by the men without resentment or patronage.

While the organisations were still able to function legally, impetus to the growing strength and importance of the women's role was given by the founda-tion of the multi-racial Federation of South African Women which had the two-fold effect of joining the demands of the African women (the strongest and largest group throughout the ANC Women's League) to those of other groups of women; and of bringing problems affecting the position of women as such to the forefront.

The strength of the Federation rested largely on the Women's Leagues in the black townships, particularly in the Transvaal and Western Cape. But Indian, Coloured and white women were also active in the Federation, whose secretary, Helen Joseph, was a white woman, and president the dynamic black woman, Lilian Ngoyi. Over the years the Federation organised women for specific struggles of their own in the townships, concerning food prices, housing, education and the children.

The Federation was unable to continue its activities after all its leading members had been placed under house arrest and banning orders, and when the ANC itself was banned in 1960 the Women's League became illegal. Leading

54

women not only lived for years under stringent banning orders but were even prohibited from talking to each other.

The last few years have seen many signs of the deepening of black consciousness in South Africa, manifesting itself particularly in the student's movement through the all-black South African Students' Organisation and other groups such as the Black Peoples Convention (BPC) and the Black Community Programme, all founded since 1970 and subsequently the object of repeated official harassment and repression. Among the 32 blacks associated with SASO, the BPC, etc., who were served with banning orders during 1973 was Mrs Sumboornam Moodley, a former high school teacher dismissed by the Indian Affairs Department, who was working as a research assistant for the Black Community Programme. Also banned was Mrs Ela Ramgobin, a social worker and vice president of the Natal Indian Congress (her husband is also banned).

In the last half of 1974 a prohibited rally called in Durban to celebrate the inauguration of the Frelimo-led transitional government in Mozambique was followed by widespread raids and arrests among leaders and supporters of the various Black Consciousness groups, many of whom were unconnected with the rally. The raids and detentions took place over several months, from September 1974 to February 1975; those involved included 13 charged under the Terrorism Act, 18 charged under the Riotous Assemblies Act, and about 40 held in detention for indefinite periods. Of the last, Mrs Brigette Mabandla was held for 171 days before being released and reunited with her baby daughter and husband (also detained). Also detained for many weeks was Mrs Vino Cooper, 25-year old member of the Theatre Council of Natal (a black progressive group promoting experimental theatre) and BPC supporter. Her husband was in detention at the same time and continued to be held after her release in November 1974.[40]

In 1975, during International Women's Year, a new Black Women's Federation was established with the object of linking black groups in practical activities. They compiled a booklet informing African women of their legal rights and launched a scheme to slash the expense of compulsory school uniforms of black pupils by buying material wholesale, making it up and selling direct to parents, who already have to pay for books and other contributions towards their children's education, out of very limited incomes.

One of the moving forces in the Black Women's Federation was Fatima Meer, first black President of the Association of Sociologists of Southern Africa, university lecturer and author. At an international gathering of the Methodist Church in the United States, Fatima Meer—the only South African present and a Muslim at that—told delegates that she realised the true potential power of women as a force for change, with the problems of racism and sexism inextricably linked. "In both", she said, "physical characteristics are used as an excuse for discrimination and domination. If we truly succeed in bringing into focus discrimination against black women, then in one single stroke we will also have focused attention on race discrimination".

As a result of her activities, Fatima Meer received a banning order that confined her to Durban and prohibited her from publishing or being quoted. She was also refused a passport to travel abroad. In August of 1976, together with her son and her son-in-law, she was detained following the uprising. In October 1977 the Black Women's Federation was banned together with 17 other organisations.

There has also been increasing activity on the economic front with waves of strikes (all illegal) involving large numbers of workers. Reflecting the occupational structure, the majority of strikers are men, but women, as already described, have always been at the forefront of those organising and participating in trade union activity. Many women workers have been active in the recent upsurge of protest against low wages and appalling working conditions. The insecurity of their position and the pitifully low pay they receive makes their actions all the more courageous.

At the end of January 1973 22 women working at a textile weaving and mending mill in New Germany went on strike; their basic weekly wage was R4.50 (£3). The same day 300 African and Indian women sorters at a Pinetown woolwashing mill refused a derisory pay rise on wages of R6.35 (£4) a week and were sent home. At the end of February 200 women packers at a canning factory in the border area of Empangeni walked out in protest against their low wages (R3 per week — under £2) and were joined by the men workers. These are only a few examples.[41]

Soweto and After

In June 1976 a demonstration of schoolchildren protesting against the enforced use of Afrikaans in their schools began a chain of events that rapidly became a national uprising against apartheid.

It is not necessary here to describe the heroic and tragic events that started in Soweto and spread to towns and townships throughout South Africa, but simply to record that girls and women were prominent in all phases of the uprising; there were probably more female participants in 1976 than in any previous manifestation of struggle.

This was seen in the photographs of the students on their protest marches, with girls in their old-fashioned gym-slips well to the fore; in the very large numbers of women held as detainees under the new Internal Security Act; and in the grim evidence of the mortuaries, where parents sought the bodies of their daughters as well as their sons.

It was a black woman journalist, Sophie Tema, who gave the world the first eye-witness account of the initial police massacre of the children. And during the three days and nights of unrelieved horror that followed, as well as during subsequent weeks while clashes continued, it was a group of women members, of the Black Women's Federation, who organised in the most practical way possible. They went into the thick of the fighting to try to help families. As they drove round the township, groups of children told them where they would find the dead and the injured. These women went into a nightmare of smoke and shooting to help other women find their children, often dead or hideously wounded, sometimes blinded or paralysed by gunshot.

Among those identified as 'agitators' and flung into detention as the upsurge continued were a number of well-known figures: Winnie Mandela—once again; Fatima Meer the sociologist; Joyce Seroke, of the South African YWCA; Sally Motlana, vice-president of the SA Council of Churches; Dr. Mamphela Ramphele, from a black health clinic in the Eastern Cape; Dimza Pityana, of the SA Institute of Race Relations, and many other professional women prominent in their communities—social workers, nurses, teachers, churchwomen, journalists. One of those to suffer most was Lindiwe Sisulu, daughter of Walter Sisulu, the ANC leader serving a life sentence on Robben Island; she was held for over a year under the Terrorism Act and cruelly treated.

Mpho Thoeaebale was a 16 year old Soweto student who lived through the events of 1976—the original decision to boycott classes and the planning of the march on 16 June, when she saw many of her friends killed or wounded. The police violence prompted the students to further demonstrations against buildings and beerhalls owned by the government; they appealed to their parents to stay away from work and join in their demonstrations. Mpho was arrested herself, held incommunicado for six weeks, during which she was beaten in attempts to make her 'confess' to sabotage or turn state's witness against her friends, and finally released, when she fled the country. She is one of a large number of young people who have left South Africa to carry on the struggle outside.

While black women were in this way taking a very active part in the events of 1976, white women reacted in a different way, by forming an organisation called Women for Peace. This group was convened by Mrs. Harry Oppenheimer, wife of the gold and diamond millionaire, and other white women who had been shocked and disturbed by the shooting of schoolchildren. A large number of women flocked to the first meeting, where they heard first-hand accounts of the massacres, such as that from Mrs. Sally Khali of a Soweto nursery creche, whose tiny charges saw police shoot down eight children on the open space next to the creche.

The genuine feelings of such white women are not to be doubted, nor their sincere desire to meet black women in an attempt to improve race relations. But a searching light needs to be thrown on the actual results of their efforts to bring friendship and peace between white and black. For what did they do? The first forms of action were deputations to government ministers, on the grounds that their aim was to create trust between Women for Peace and those in power. That is, to act as a buffer between the militancy of the students and the power of the state, which turns the guns of its police onto children.

Women for Peace also prayed publicly for peace, fearing the outcome of deepening strife. But black women cannot pray for peace; they will have to fight for it. And the forms of organisation which ultimately unite black and white women in action for a better life will arise not in the white suburbs but in the black townships, where black women know the reality of apartheid and the means to overthrow it.

CHAPTER 10

Looking Forward

The past three decades in South Africa have been years of rapid economic and political change. A quarter century of Nationalist party rule has been responsible for the systematic denial of black aspirations whether political, social or economic and for the introduction of ever more repressive legislation and security methods. The black people, in their turn, have passed from conventional political organisation and protest, which was answered by violence, persecution and imprisonment, to new forms of protest and resistance, and to clandestine organisation directed at eventual armed struggle for the liberation of their country.

On the economic front these changes have been accompanied by industrial and commercial development that has brought great prosperity to white South Africa. The white population now enjoys one of the highest standards of living in the world; measured in purely material terms, white women in particular have attained a life of exceptional privilege and ease.

The vast majority of African women have also seen their lives undergo substantial changes in recent decades, but they have not progressed towards a better life. On the contrary, their position is worse than it has ever been. Always the greatest victims of an oppressive and racist system, they are today even greater victims in a system whose anomalies increase.

It is easy to understand that the question of power is central to black liberation in South Africa, and for this absolutely basic reason, no 'reform' of apartheid can ever radically alter the position of the black majority. But it is not so easily accepted by men that the question of power is central, too, to women's liberation, and thus for women as well, reform can never be the answer.

In many ways the instability of life of black South Africans is forcing the women to exert greater strength and show higher qualities of character than the men. Sociologists have commented on the emergence of the single, independent black woman. Professor Monica Wilson, of the University of Cape Town, speaking recently on the 'Changing Status of African Women' said that the rights of African women in the Republic were destroyed more by the fact that they were part of a disenfranchised community than that they were women. "The most pressing disability of African women is the restriction of movement and residence which prevents them from living with their husbands. Because of this many educated African women were rejecting marriage altogether. Why be tied to a man who because of his work is continually absent?" The right of a woman to live with her husband at his place of work and to enjoy the family life was the very basis of society. "I cannot feel that any other limitations on the rights of African women are of comparable importance."[42]

A black newspaper editor, Mr Tom Moerane, reports on research undertaken by his daughter among African women. "A significant number of young women regarded marriage in an entirely negative manner. They said they did not care about marriage as an institution nor did they think it was of any particular use to them. Some indicated that they desired to bear children and that this made it necessary to cohabit with a man, but 'the baby is going to be my baby.' . . . The main reason for this attitude seemed to be that young urban women regarded men as totally irresponsible. I myself, through my own observations, have to believe that the women in the urban communities are very much more responsible and more practical.

"Successful families appear to be those where the women have the responsibility for the vital and basic necessities of living . . . the women bear the brunt. My daughter maintains that urban black societies are becoming matriarchal in character."[43]

Migrant labour has long distorted the clearly defined roles of male and female in tribal society as in industrial society. In the reserves women must do what was once the men's traditional work — ploughing for instance — where in the past it was considered wrong and shameful for either to do the other's work.

Man has lost his position in tribal society of being the protector of the family, responsible for its welfare within a stable community. He enters the new industrialised urban setting which is bewildering in its radical differences, although he could adjust to this. More important is the fact that he who is a man now becomes, in the white man's domain, a 'boy', both in name and practice.

The attitude of the dominant people in the new society, the employers, foremen, police, administrative officials, is such as to make him a boy and dehumanise him. Not only is he humiliated by this, but his own family see him treated as a 'boy'. "Our sons now despise us for accepting this position."

Women on the other hand, are protected to a certain extent from this traumatic experience. The employment they undertake is only different in degree; their role is the same whether they are in a tribal or urban situation. They still bring up their children, care for their homes and very often their work situation is only an extension of these duties to other people's homes and children, whereas a man may well feel a fear of the unfamiliar job he has to do. "The dehumanisation of the black man is not a problem of urbanisation or industrialisation. It is a problem of race and colour and the racial policy by which we are all ruled."[44]

The black man is in fact denied the power he once had of being head of his own family. The women become the heads.

Unmarried mothers, widows, divorcees and deserted wives form a significant part of the female population. A large number support themselves and are in fact, if not in law, the heads of independent households.

Migrant labour and resettlement camps place on the women the total responsibility and burden of management of home and children. For long years the woman alone holds together the remnants of the family. For the man, his children are strangers to him, growing up without his discipline or his loving assistance. The woman is forced into an extraordinary kind of independence, bitter and painful, but calling forth qualities of strength and endurance. Lonely, impoverished and deprived as she is, she still remains the pivot of such life as the family has left to them, shouldering her immense burdens with unbelievable fortitude and tremendous tenacity.

In debarring women from the towns, the white government gives tacit recognition to this primary position of women who by their very presence and stability would destroy the myths of apartheid.

"Women carry a double burden of disabilities. They are discriminated against on the grounds of both sex and race. The two kinds of discrimination interact and reinforce each other. A reform of personal law would not emancipate the women unless it were accompanied by such radical changes as a dissolution of tribal social relations, the spread of education, the absorption of women in remunerative occupations outside the home, and participation in the work of government. But advance on all fronts is held up by barriers erected to maintain the prerogatives and privileges of the dominant white minority.

"Colour bars retard the process of female emancipation by impeding the progress of the whole race. Women therefore choose to fight along with their men for full civic rights, rather than against the men for legal and social equality. By taking part in the national movement against racial discrimination, women have established a claim to equality. This can become a reality, however, only when both women and men have become full citizens in a free society."[45]

In other countries, whether industrially advanced or newly emerging nations such as those on other parts of the African continent, women are now raising the banners of their demands in the widespread feminist revolution, and are battering down the doors closed to them and overturning male privilege. Whether they link their just demands with a challenge to the structure of their own societies, or whether they see them simply in terms of a change in status and in male consciousness, the fact remains that they can achieve substantial advances. The changes in the legal position of women, their conditions of work, and in their own consciousness during the past decade are witness to the new revolution among the women.

In South Africa, the oppression of women has a further dimension, the dimension of apartheid. This, based partly on fantasies of racial superiority and partly on the labour requirements of an industrial capitalist society, has created an environment for women that is unique in our time.

Thus for example, although women in modern society have been repeatedly told that their place is in the home, this is a concept which has developed only with the industrial revolution when divisions between the home and the workplace first came into being. However, in South Africa, the reduction of women to 'superfluous appendages' robs them of even the limited importance given to women under ordinary capitalist-productive relationships. The creation of a home centred around the family is not necessary for women under apartheid. The whole sentimental conception: the eternal female and mother serving her husband, caring for his needs and those of her children, painted in such false and romantic colours, falls to the ground. The only function left to the black woman is through the system of reproduction (a biological fact that apartheid has not been able to change, and even this must be limited to ease the fears of whites who find themselves so numerically inferior).

The extremely high infant mortality rates are not only a source of great suffering and deprivation for black women, but also a source of their further oppression. For the result is far more pregnancies — far more periods of physical hardship during which work, education or development outside the home become impossible. For the typical white mother, pregnancy occupies no more than two or three years of her life. For the black mother, it must occupy many times that amount. And thus biology becomes yet another disability, reinforcing her inferior position.

Black women also suffer from the fact that some white men wish to exert their sexual power over both white and black women, as the prosecutions under the Immorality Act show. At the same time, they like to create the fantasy of 'pure' white womanhood, which the black man longs to defile.

And moreover, the black woman finds her role of motherhood reduced to that of a domestic nanny caring for white children while her own know only separation, suffering and neglect; the most intimate care and feeding of the white babies is handed over to black women. The extraordinary thing is that all the separation from her own children and hardships suffered by the black domestic has not deprived her of her ability to show tenderness and love in the care she gives to the children who are not hers.

The contrast with the white woman is overwhelming. White women in apartheid society are less than nothing. After parturition, the white mother is scarcely needed at all. Limited as the role of middle-class motherhood may be in other countries; in South Africa it becomes nothing; the mother is not essential to the smooth running of the home, the domestic role is played by the black domestics.

The primary role of white women becomes that of consumer and as a living display, through leisure and adornment, of her husband's wealth. The sad thing is that, freed from the destructively time-consuming and repetitive domestic chores that chain women of other lands, the white woman in South Africa is unable to utilise her freedom constructively and dissipates it in a trivial round of social activities — though there are of course notable exceptions, including those who have been persecuted for their opposition to apartheid and, to a lesser extent, the women of the Black Sash.

In South Africa black women, these most vulnerable of all people within the apartheid state, have been forced to embark on a struggle that takes them beyond their own specific oppression. The struggle of South African women for recognition as equal citizens with equal opportunities is primarily the struggle against apartheid, for national liberation. Nor is it a question of putting one first, then taking up the other. The victory of this struggle against apartheid is the absolute condition for any change in the social status of women as a whole; their participation is an expression not only of their desire to rid all South Africa of the curse of apartheid, but also of their deep concern for their own status as women.

And they have shown repeatedly the capacity to understand and the willingness to fight for changes that lift them further than their own very harsh immediate predicament.

Thus under the conditions of apartheid South Africa's oppressed women cannot limit their objectives to those of simply trying to establish their legal rights in a modern industrialised society, nor can they hope to emerge with a few privileges in what is still largely a male-dominated world; but to destroy the whole basis of racial exploitation, and in so doing open up the prospect of a free development for both women and men. In this they are an example to women's movements everywhere, for they know that the liberation of women is not simply a matter of amending laws or changing male attitudes, but of a fundamental re-structuring of a whole society towards the aims of freedom and justice for all.

Brief Biographies
Women in the Struggle

LILIAN NGOYI joined the Women's League of the African National Congress in 1952, moved by the sight of young boys going to jail during the Defiance Campaign. Her whole life had been a struggle against poverty; she went to work after only a year in high school to support her asthmatic father, her mother and brother. She became a skilled garment worker, and when she joined the Congress she was forty, a widow, with her own child, an adopted child, and her mother to support.

Her flair for public speaking and brilliant personality thrust her into the front ranks of political activity. In a year she was elected as president of the Women's League, and later became president of the Federation of South African Women.

A trip abroad to an international conference strengthened and deepened her commitment. She stood open-mouthed in an English street at the sight of white women scrubbing their own doorsteps. The tour abroad made a deep impression and when she returned huge audiences in the townships listened spellbound to her descriptions of her experience for two or three hours at a time. She was a most eloquent and colourful speaker, but this and her energy as an organiser made her a target for persecution and prosecution. In 1956 she was arrested and charged in the mammoth treason trial that did not end until more than four years later. She described her worst experience, however, as 71 days in solitary confinement when she was detained under the 90-day law.

Lilian Ngoyi was placed under severe bans and restrictions that confined her to her home in Orlando Township and prohibited her from having visitors at her home. She was forced to give up her job and tried to make a living from sewing at home, although the Special Branch scared her customers away.

After eleven years of bans and house arrest the bans were not renewed. In an interview she said "I must say I had a tough time, but my spirits have not been dampened," and then she stood up and declared "You can tell my friends all over the world that this girl is still her old self, if not more mature after all the experiences. I am looking forward to the day when my children will share in the wealth of our lovely South Africa."

ELIZABETH MAFEKENG, an extraordinarily young-looking mother of eleven children, was a vice-President of the ANC Women's League and an indefatigable trade union organizer. Because of her brave and successful fight on behalf of African trade unions she was banished from her home in the Cape to a remote area, where she was forced to live in isolation without her husband and children. She managed to escape to Lesotho (then Basutoland), where she settled, but her family was never re-united and she has endured much hardship and loneliness.

FRANCINA BAARD, a former leader of the ANC, a leading member of the Food and Canning Workers' Union and of SACTU's Local and Management Committees, was forced to leave her home and her family in Port Elizabeth when she was sent into banishment in Mabopane, in the Transvaal.

One morning in 1948 as she walked to work, she saw men lying in puddles of water because they had nowhere to sleep. "I wept and resolved that something had to be done." She went to an ANC meeting, and joined.

Soon she was organising the Women's League, and so she was arrested in the big 1956 swoop, and put on trial for treason. She was detained in 1960, and in 1963 she was again arrested and kept in solitary confinement for a year before her trial. "I nearly went off my mind".

She served five years in prison for contravening the Suppression of Communism Act, and was released in 1969. Then she had to part with her children once more, as she was banished to Mabopane, a place where she had no relatives and knew nobody. "I will never forget my first night there. I was taken to an old two-roomed corrugated iron shack. All I had on me were the clothes I had worn when arrested. There was no furniture, no curtains. It was a bitterly cold night and I had to sleep on the floor dressed only in my jersey and my dress."

She found a job, but her employer could not register her, because Francina Baard absolutely refused to take a pass. Eventually the authorities issued one to her which she took under protest.

After many long years, the banishment order was lifted, but she has not returned to her home. When she was banished the municipality evicted her children from their house. Now the family is scattered. There is no home left in Port Elizabeth, and she has made her home at Mabopane. "Like all mothers I would like to have my children with me but you cannot always have things your way."

Her life has been hard. Her husband died in 1953. Now she is unable to work because of leg trouble, and her son sends her what he can from Johannesburg. She is over sixty and not able to move around, but her indestructible spirit remains. She says, "I have survived."

HELEN JOSEPH went to India from England, where she was born, to teach in a school for girls. Later she taught in Durban, married, served as an officer in the women's forces during the war, and came to Johannesburg where she began working for the Medical Aid Society of the non-racial Garment Workers' Union. This was the beginning of her political involvement. She joined the Congress of Democrats, and became Secretary of the Women's Federation.

A tremendous organiser with a formidable capacity for sheer hard work, Helen Joseph played a key role in organising the democratic protests of South African women against apartheid and against passes for women. She was arrested in 1956, and endured the endless court appearances of the treason trial to its very end. The ANC asked her to serve on a welfare committee that was appointed to

Lilian Ngoyi

Albertina Sisulu

Florence Matomela

Elizabeth Mafekeng

Dorothy Nyembe

Francina Baard

Mary Moodley

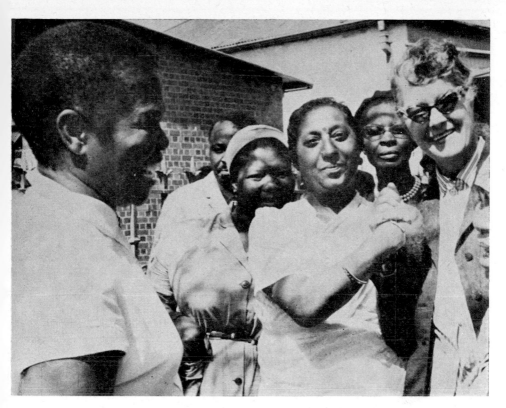

Helen Joseph with Thayanaygii Pillay and Lilian Ngoyi

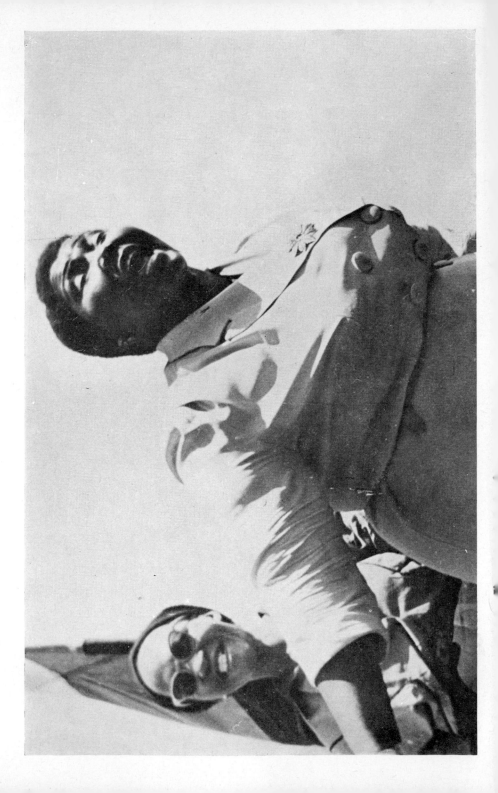

assist political exiles. She has written a most moving account of her visits to those in banishment in her book 'Tomorrow's Sun'.

Helen Joseph was the first person to be put under house arrest in South Africa after the promulgation of the new law. She lived alone, and endured ten continuous years of stringent conditions, without being permitted visitors, confined to her home every evening and all weekends, not permitted to leave Johannesburg for a brief holiday, and silenced by bans.

After an operation for cancer, the ten-year house arrest orders were not renewed. Undaunted by her persecution, Helen Joseph has since spoken at students' meetings and continues to speak against apartheid. Her pride, her integrity, her devotion and splendid organising abilities have made her famous beyond the borders of her own country.

NONSIKELELO ALBERTINA SISULU has maintained her home and brought up and educated her own five children, together with two children of her deceased sister, while her husband serves life imprisonment on Robben Island. She has not only kept the family financially through her work as a nurse and midwife, but has played a notable part in the political life of her country and people. She was prominent in both the ANC Women's League and the Women's Federation, and worked closely with Lilian Ngoyi. She has often been subject to tremendous pressures, particularly when her husband Walter Sisulu (formerly national secretary of the ANC) was in hiding from the police before his arrest at Rivonia. She was often interrogated and threatened by the police, and she and her eldest son Max, then 16, were arrested and held under the 90-days law in an attempt to force them to reveal the whereabouts of Walter Sisulu.

She endured long years of banning orders and house arrest, but has still managed to get her children educated, and is always remembered for her calm, strong, quiet personality, the very epitome of the endurance and steadfastness of the women of South Africa.

MARY MOODLEY is still 'Auntie Mary' to thousands of men, women and children in Wattville township in Benoni; there is no way of describing her warm-hearted personality, but all the persecuted and lonely people in her district came to Auntie Mary for comfort and for help.

Living in squalid Wattville, with its run-down streets and thin shabby children, over the years she plunged deeper and deeper into work to help all those suffering around her. A solid supporter of the Congress and trade union movement, she took the fight for a better life to every apartheid official, was arrested, banned, persecuted, yet never lost her warm-heartedness and looked after a continually growing family as waifs drifted to the shelter of her roof and were "adopted".

Her activities in the Women's Federation, on numerous local committees, and as a trade union organiser, led to her arrest in 1960. When she was released and returned home the whole township turned out to welcome her, while children ran through the streets shouting 'Auntie Mary's back! Auntie Mary's back!'

When told by the doctors that she must diet to lose weight as she suffered from heart disease, she said, "How can I sit and eat expensive meat while the children eat porridge? I eat what they eat." When she was in solitary confinement in jail, she described later how she got up off the floor and danced to keep up her spirits.

She was arrested together with her daughter for helping political refugees to escape from the country. Today she is banned and restricted, but her spirit blazes as brightly as ever.

WINNIE MANDELA has been subject to more than ten years of continuous harassment and persecution by the police. She had been active in the ANC Women's League, and became a target for the Security Police both through her own actions and as a symbol — the wife of the outstanding black leader Nelson Mandela, now serving a life sentence on Robben Island.

She was placed under banning orders that restricted her work so that she lost her job. She has been arrested and charged many times with offences concerned with breaking her banning orders. In 1969 she was arrested and held in solitary confinement under the Terrorism Act and subject to five days and nights continuous interrogation with sleep deprivation, although she suffers from a heart complaint. More than six months later she and 20 others were brought to court on charges concerned with activities of the illegal ANC. The trial came to an abrupt end two months later when the charges were withdrawn, and the accused found not guilty and discharged. They were immediately re-arrested, and Winnie Mandela endured another $5\frac{1}{2}$ months of solitary confinement before being brought to court once more in a trial that also ended in acquittal, after 491 days in prison, most of them in *absolute* solitary confinement. When her banning order expired in 1975, she was briefly free to take part in political activity once more, and travelled the country. Following the demonstrations and shootings in Soweto in 1976, however, her Orlando home was suspected of being one of the organisational bases of the uprising and she was taken again into detention until the end of the year. In what appears to have been a desperate attempt to break her determination to resist, or at least to force her into exile, the government altered Winnie Mandela's banning order in May 1977; she was removed to the small Free State town of Brandfort (or rather to the nameless location that attaches to Brandfort) several hundred miles from her home and friends. In March 1978 she was again convicted of breaking her ban and given a suspended sentence of 12 months.

FATIMA MEER, born in 1929, has taught sociology at Natal University since 1959 and is the highest-ranking black academic in a white South African university. She participated in the Defiance Campaign and in founding the Women's Federation, and was banned from 1952-4.

During the 1960's she concentrated on academic work, publishing a number of books and making trips abroad, but she continued to speak out forcefully on racial issues. In 1975 she was elected president of the Black Women's Federation (subsequently banned). In July 1976 the government refused to renew her passport; she was also detained under the Internal Security Act and banned on her release, so that although she may continue to teach, she may not publish or engage in political activity, or travel.

DR MAMPHELA RAMPHELE was born in 1948 in the Northern Transvaal and qualified in medicine at the University of Natal. In 1975 she was responsible for opening and running the Zanempilo Health Clinic at King Williams Town, a project established by the Black Community Programmes and serving a large black community, mainly the families of migrant workers. She was closely connected with Mapetla Mohapi (whose family she represented at the post-mortem and inquest) and Steve Biko, both of whom died in police custody. From August to December 1976 Dr. Ramphele was detained under the Internal Security Act and in April 1977 she was served with a banning order preventing her from carrying on her work at the clinic and removing her to a remote district in the northern Transvaal. She has been refused permission to live with her parents and in October 1977 was reported to be operating a community health project with a Catholic mission at Trichardsdal, acting as a local travelling doctor.

RITA NDZANGA lived with her husband Lawrence and four children in Soweto, and was engaged in trade union organisation. In 1969 she and Lawrence were brought to court with 19 others on a large number of political charges. She had been in solitary confinement for seven months, when not being interrogated by the security police. Later she gave a description of how she was questioned and assaulted in a blacked-out room. She was made to stand on a pile of bricks and questioned without respite until she collapsed: "I fell down and hit a gas-pipe . . . the same man pulled me up by my hair again . . . his hands were full of my hair. He washed his hands in a basin. They said 'On the bricks!' I stood on the bricks and they hit me again. I fell. They poured water on me. I could not stand the assault any longer. They said 'Meid, jy moet praat!' ('Girl, you must talk')." Lawrence was also brutally assaulted, but in court the case against them was dismissed. All were discharged and immediately re-arrested and put back into solitary confinement.

This second period of detention lasted $5\frac{1}{2}$ months. Then they were brought to trial again, and again acquitted. Late in 1976, Rita and Lawrence were again acquitted. Late in 1976, Rita and Lawrence were again taken into police custody. The day she was due to appear in court, charged again on political charges, she was informed that her husband was dead. He was one of the horrifying number of detainees to die at the hands of the police. Rita was not released on bail until it was too late for her to attend the funeral; she was then tried under the Terrorism Act, and again acquitted.

Women in Jail

DOROTHY NYEMBE born in 1930, joined the ANC in her early twenties and became a women's organiser in the ANC. During the Defiance Campaign she served two prison sentences; in 1956 she led the contingent of Natal women who protested against the pass laws in Pretoria, in August. In 1959 she was endorsed out of Durban. During the 1960 State of Emergency she was detained for five months.

In 1962 she represented the Women's Federation at a conference on labour problems called by SACTU and the Natal Rural Areas Committee. In 1963 she was arrested, charged with furthering the aims of the ANC and sentenced to three years imprisonment. First banned for five years in 1963, she was re-banned in 1968.

In 1968 Dorothy Nyembe was again detained (with eleven others) and in February 1969 charged in Pietermaritzburg under the Terrorism Act and the Suppression of Communism Act, accused of harbouring freedom fighters and assisting two co-defendants. In March 1969 she was sentenced to 15 years imprisonment; originally in the Barberton Women's Prison, she was recently transferred to Kroonstad Prison.

Dorothy Nyembe is unmarried. She is due for release in 1984. There is no remission for political prisoners in South Africa.

EDITH THENJIWA MBALA, aged 50, was employed in Johannesburg as a switchboard operator when she was arrested and charged in September 1976 under the Suppression of Communism Act. It was alleged that during the uprising she had reproduced an ANC pamphlet entitled "Amandla Soweto" on a photocopier with the intention of distributing it. She was convicted in March 1977 of furthering the aims of the ANC and sentenced to three years' imprisonment. She is due for release in 1980.

MAGOTAKE ESTHER MALEKA was born in 1943, the eldest of seven children and the daughter of an ANC militant. After her father went into exile in 1964 and her mother died in 1965, Esther took over the care of her six brothers and sisters, acting as a real parent to them until the day of her arrest. She became actively involved in politics while still at school, and was arrested in March 1976 together with a number of other young people. In December 1976 she was brought to trial with David Thathe, husband to one of her sisters, and charged with recruiting others to join the ANC forces for military training abroad. Two young men had been arrested trying to cross into Botswana without passports and through torture police extracted the information that Esther had been responsible for organising recruits. Both Esther and David were convicted and sentenced to five years' imprisonment. She has two young children who are being looked after by relatives, and is due to be released at the end of 1981.

HAPPY JOYCE MASHAMBA was born in 1950 and trained in librarianship. She is the mother of two young children and wife of T. Godwin Mashamba, philosophy lecturer at the University of the North at Turfloop, where she was also working, as a library assistant, at the time of her arrest in May 1976. Her husband and two other men were also arrested, and all four were brought to trial in October 1976 charged with being members of the ANC and furthering its aims by recruiting students and other activities. On 28 June 1977 Mrs. Mashamba was convicted, together with her husband and two other men, and sentenced to five years' imprisonment. She will be released in 1982.

Appendix

AFRICAN WOMEN—FACTS & FIGURES

Total African population (1970) 15,036,360

Females 7,649,020

Table I

Where they live

| | Africans | |
	Females	Total (M & F)
in black rural areas (reserves)	3,719,480	6,409,780
in white urban areas	1,866,280	4,370,220
in white rural areas	1,768,860	3,662,980
in black urban areas (Bantustan towns)	294,400	593,380

(*Population census* 6 *May* 1970 *Dept. of Statistics Report* 02-02-02)

Table II

Occupation (Sample tabulation)

| | Africans | | |
	males	females	%
Professional workers	37,200	56,100	3.0
Administrative workers	3,300	100	.0
Clerical workers	88,900	7,380	.4
Sales workers	92,800	18,080	1.0
Service workers	295,240	716,700	38.0
Agricultural workers	1,397,280	654,320	34.6
Production & Transport workers	608,720	80,120	4.0
Unclassifiable	193,100	355,800	19.0
Total economically active	3,716,540	1,888,600	100.0%
Not economically active	3,670,800	5,760,420	

(*ibid.*)

Table III

Employment in the Bantu Homelands (women)

Occupation	No.
Professional	27,380
Administrative	80
Clerical, etc.	1,500
Sales, etc.	6,140
Services	81,220
Farming	411,380
Production and transport	20,460
Unclassified	157,020
Total economically active	705,180
Total female population	4,013,880

(ibid.)

Table IV

Blacks and whites in selected occupations

		Male	Female
University teachers:	White	5,404	1,118
	African	99	11
School teachers:	White	20,907	33,846
	African	27,202	29,663
Doctors:	White	7,779	665
	African	65	4
Nurses	White	852	13,268
	African	1,018	12,407
Pharmacists:	White	3,450	764
	African	37	—
Chemists:	White	1,082	136
	African	13	—
Architects:	White	1,768	88
	African	—	—
Lawyers	White	4,038	25
	African	211	—
Librarians:	White	213	808
	African	15	13
Clerks & Typists:	White	47,144	157,936
	African	18,576	2,123

(Dept. of Labour Manpower Survey 27.4.73)

Table V
African Teachers' Salaries p.a. (as from 1.4.74)

	Male	Female
Head of large secondary school	R4,089–5,288	R3,525–4,759
Teacher with degree	R2,115–3,525	R1,904–3,102
Qualified teacher	R1,163–2,538	R 987–1,798
Unqualified teacher	R 987	R 917

(*SAIRR Annual Survey* 1974 *p*. 349)

Table VI
African cotton textile workers' wages p.w. (as from 9.7.75)

	Male	Female
Main urban areas		
Grade One	R15.00	R12.00
Grade Two (max)	R16.50	R13.20
Grade Three (max)	R18.00	R14.40
Grade Four (max)	R21.00	R16.80
Border areas		
Grade One	R12.00	R 9.60
Grade Two (max)	R13.20	R10.60
Grade Three (max)	R14.40	R11.50
Grade Four (max)	R16.50	R13.20

(*Bantu Labour Regulations Order No. R2379*, 14.12.73)

References

Two major sources of information on African women in South Africa, which have been extensively drawn on here, are:

H.J. Simons, *African Women: their Legal Status in South Africa* (London, 1968)

Elizabeth S. Landis, *Apartheid and the Disabilities of African Women in South Africa* (UN Unit on Apartheid, December 1973).

1. Address by Mr G. F. van L. Froneman, Deputy Chairman of the Bantu Affairs Commission to the Institute of Citizenship, in Cape Town on 30 May 1968 and subsequently published by the Dept. of Information.

2. *A Place Called Dimbaza* (Africa Publications Trust, London, 1973).

3. House of Assembly Debates, 6.2.68.

4. Debates, 23.5.69.

5. Debates, 24.4.68.

6. Debates, 17.3.64.

7. *Black Sash*, 1974.

8. Francis Wilson, *Migrant Labour in South Africa* (Johannesburg, 1972).

9. *A Place Called Dimbaza*, op. cit.

10. Debates, 4.2.69.

11. Debates, 6.2.68.

12. Ferdinand Mount, "The Sense of Dispossession" *Encounter* (December 1972).

13. Bruno Bettelheim, *The Informed Heart* (London, 1961).

14. Trudi Thomas, "Sowing seeds of deprivation", *Black Sash* (May 1974).

15. Simons, op. cit. The three quotations that follow are from this source.

16. Debates, 6.3.62.

17. Landis, op. cit.

18. Simons, op. cit.

19. ibid.

20. Phyllis Ntantala, "African Tragedy" *Africa South* Vol. 1 No. 3 (1957).

21. Cosmas Desmond, *The Discarded People* (Christian Institute, 1971).

22. ibid.

23. *Rand Daily Mail*, 3.4.67.

24. *Natal Witness*, 3.4.67.

25. Sally Motlana, "The Laws which humiliate", *Black Sash* (June 1972).

26. ibid.

27. Thomas, op. cit.

28. ibid.

29. ibid.

30. Quoted in Sheena Duncan, "The illegal children", *Black Sash* (Feb 1973)

31. Wilson, op. cit.

32. Simons, op. cit.

33. For a full account, see Charles Hooper, *Brief Authority* (London 1960).

34. Sol Plaatje, *Native Life in South Africa* (Penguin 1969).

35. Mary Benson, *Struggle for a Birthright* (Penguin 1966).

36. Hooper, op. cit.

37. Hilda Bernstein, *The Terrorism of Torture* (IDAF 1972).

38. ibid.

39. Quoted in Mary Benson, *Purge of the Eastern Cape* (Christian Action).

40. See "3rd Report on Arrests, Detentions and Trials" Programme for Social Change, Braamfontein 18.4.75.

41. *The Durban Strikes* 1973, Institute for Industrial Education (Durban 1974).

42. *Cape Times*, 9.5.74.

43. *Black Sash*, August 1973.

44. ibid.

45. Simons, op. cit.

Printed by A. G. Bishop & Sons Ltd., Orpington, Kent.